When The Light Changed Me

True story
by
Jennie Ortiz

Copyright © 2008 by Jennie A Ortiz

Cover created by Jennie A Ortiz

Pictures are copyright

All rights reserved

This story is nonfiction

Authorjennieo@gmail.com

This book is dedicated to

Jesus Christ

and

Blanca Enelida Vazquez

TABLE OF CONTENTS

Thank you note i
Special note ii
When my life began to change 1
Family history 4
My grandmother Blanca 6
The story of Conchita's kids and grandkids 9
The Christmas Story 10
When my parents meet 12
The family story 17
The news of Eliza Muñez 19
The move to Boston Mass 20
A dedication to my mother 22
While growing up 24
My time in high school 26
My time in Bangor, Maine 30
The start of the unknown, my spiritual Path 33
Mental illness struck our family 39
The death of my best friend 42
Family comes together once again 45
When my life started to change 48
Seeing Auras and sparkles 58
Medium Reading 75
Grandmother 81
My trip to Sabana Grande 90
One of my first dream Prediction 95
Seen and feeling things around me 97
The year I will never forget 102
When the light changed me 105
Still looking for reason 127
Learning about Medium and Psychics 131
First words with a Spirit Guide 137
Laura told me her experience 140
Uneasy feeling 142
What I went through 144
A different outlook 150

Religion	155
Having a dream	161
Thinking Positive	164
Still learning about Herminio	167
What ever happened to the little boy?	170
The Metaphysical group	172
Doreen's Story	179
Yaya's Story	182
Looking back on the family tree	185
Advice	187
Predictions	188
My final thought	189
Let the "Light" of Jesus light your way	190
In memory of	191

THANK YOU NOTE

First of all, I want to thank JESUS, without Him this book would have never been possible. I want to thank my mother, Blanca E Vazquez, for giving her all being a mother and father, to me and my brother to raise us the best she could. Also, my brother Ferdie Ortiz thanks for all your support. I also want to thank, Bertha, Dorothy Leered, Lois Stewart, Buddy, Joyce Seyer and Becky. And for everyone that supported me when my door changed in my home. Carmelina, Joan Almeida, Mayra, Melissa Rodriguez, Maria Rodriguez, Iris Santiago, Connie Vazquez, Yvonne Hernandez, Edermira Colon, Ariel Gonzalez, Nylia Arce, Adianez Gonzalez, Helen Hernandez, Maria Vazquez, Leonor Hernandez, Hollis and her family, Blondie and her family Maria Anaya and her entire family, Marie Ortiz, Liz McCall, and Doreen Wales. For those that helped me with your spiritual gifts, Marie Ortiz, Jacki Joy, Edermira Colon, Joyce Seyer, Cesar, Yamir Mendez, Lillian Hernandez. And a special thank you so much to Katiria Montero for all your help. I also want to thank all that are helping me with your spiritual gifts. God Bless you.

For the Metaphysical group, I thank you all for your help. Pamela Sayre, Doreen Wales, Jennifer Thomas, and the rest of the members thank you. For those I could not name, too many names to keep going, you know who you are. God bless you all from New Hampshire to Massachusetts, to New York City, Oklahoma and Puerto Rico.

Thank you

SPECIAL NOTE

A special thanks to everyone who is about to read this book. This message is for everyone who has had a paranormal experience at any time in your life. If you think you are alone in the world and that you don't have anyone to back you up, then think again, you are not alone. I'm letting you know that there are a lot of people who feel the same way. There are a lot of people who have gone through many similar experiences of paranormal or spiritual basis.

I want you all to know that this book is a true story. The book is about religion. Jesus Christ and the Virgin Mary are named in this book. This book also has religious pictures and family pictures. When I began my journey, I felt the need to go back to the family tree and find out who else had experienced the paranormal or went through a spiritual journey like I had.

I want people to know that the children's names have been changed for their safety. Sit back and enjoy this book; God bless you and your family. My name is Jennie and at the age of 40 I decided to write this book because Jesus Christ and the Virgin Mary came into my life. This is my story.

When my life began to change

Before I tell my story, I have to say I never thought at the age of forty, I'd be the one in my family to be writing a book. I was raised in Dorchester, Massachusetts. I went to public school and graduated from Madison Park High in 1986. At the age of eighteen, I left Dorchester and moved to Bangor, Maine, where I stayed for two and a half years. In 1990 while I was living in Bangor, my mother, Nellie, and my brother Ferdie, moved to New Hampshire. When I finished school, I moved to Portland, Maine for a short time. Later, I decided to move back home with my mother and this is my story.

On January 28, 2008, at noon, I went to my mother's house and we were having a conversation. She then brought to my attention that in August 2007, I was acting strange, and my eyes were wide open like I'd seen a ghost or something. She said I was acting so strange that she became very worried about me because I looked like I was lost. I explained to her why I never told her what happened to me that summer of 2007. So, I decided to tell her what happened and why I was acting strangely. "On July 5, 2007, at the age of thirty-nine, my life changed. It was at this time that my spiritual guide began talking to me.

I started to hear them telling me, things that's when I began to write everything down that the spirit guide was telling me. At the time I didn't know I was writing down predictions. One of the predictions was that the Boston Red Sox would win the 2007 World Series. Much to my surprise, the prediction came true. At this exact moment, I could hear my spiritual guide clearly.

However, on July 25, 2007, instead of one voice I began to hear many voices, all at once, telling me over and over, "***HE'S COMING! HE'S COMING!***" I didn't know what to think, I was terrified and thought, "***Oh my God! I'm hearing so many 'voices.'*** I was scared and I didn't know who to turn to for help. I began to cry and I started to go to all the Catholic churches, I could find. I felt that I needed some kind "protection." I was so scared and panicked. While in my state of fear, I kept running from church to church for protection.

Through all the panic and crying I was going through, I wondered why didn't I think of asking the spirit guide why was I hearing so many voices? Meanwhile, I sat in an empty church crying and praying for help, and at home, I cried even more. "Then on August 1, 2007, I decided to go to Pepperell, Massachusetts, which has an altar of the statue of Fatima and a big picture frame of JESUS and other Saints. While I knelt down in front of the big picture frame of Jesus Christ, I started to cry. I began to pray to Jesus Christ, asking Him to help me because I was so scared. When I finished praying, I happened to look next to the big picture of Jesus, where another picture of Jesus hung, except that the second picture was of only His face. I walked over to the picture, and for some reason, I touched it.

I then looked at my left hand and touched my right hand, with which I had touched the picture. I stayed for a couple of hours and then left around six or seven in the evening. I was calm and drove back home to New Hampshire. For some reason, I looked out my drivers-side window and I saw the sun and it was changing! The sun looked completely different, that's when I saw the sun's rays. They took on so many colors shining, straight down.

Red, yellow, green, brown and many other different colors were around the sun. Then the sun started to jump around like it was dancing. That's when I decided to stop the car to see it better. Then it looked like a dark moon passed over it, like an eclipse. What I saw was amazing, beautiful and surprising. What shocked me was that someone was coming towards me from the sun, and his hand was wide open. Then I realized it was Him: JESUS CHRIST! I was shocked.

He came straight towards me. He had brown hair, a brown beard, and a white robe. Then he vanished just as quickly as he appeared. I stayed parked on the side of the road for several more minutes. I could not believe what I had just seen. I was too scared to tell you, Mom, what was happening to me with the voices and then seeing "Jesus." Then on August 18, 2007, my life took another turn.

Before I tell my story, I will tell you why I'm taking you back a couple of years through my family history. "I went on a search for some answers," by searching which family member could've been a Medium or psychic themselves. Meanwhile, you will get to know who I am and where I come from.

Family history

My family comes from Puerto Rico. Eliza Muñiz was my great-great-great grandmother. She had five children, two of whom I remember. I used to visit her son Florencio Negron. And my mother always mentions her daughter, Concepcion Muñiz, because my mother's grandmother. Eliza had three other daughters: Aleja Negron, (also known as Giyermina, as well as her nickname, Gilli), and Adela Negron. Eliza was very Catholic, and she took her children to church every Sunday; she also taught them to be respectful. Concepcion also had a nickname, Conchita. When Conchita grow up, she met her first husband, Francisco Moreda. Soon after, Conchita had her daughter Antoñia Moreda.

Then her husband left her. After a while Conchita met her second husband, Pedro, and they had children: Sarah, Herminio, Delia, and in the fall of 1924, my grandmother, Blanca, was born. I do remember Growing up and seeing my great-grandmother Conchita's wooden house. It was very small with two bedrooms, a tiny kitchen, and the living room. She had many children in this small house and even though it was small she loved to cook for everyone. Pedro worked in the sugar cane field as a supervisor. Conchita used to cook for the employees, while Pedro did the "payroll" giving each employee their paycheck.

One of the men that worked for Pedro was getting paid, but he thought that Pedro didn't pay him enough money and he killed Pedro, for fifteen cents. After her husband died Conchita's fourteen-year-old son, Herminio, worked to help his mother Conchita and his four sisters.

Herminio worked carrying water to the people that worked in the sugar cane field and other places. At the age of sixteen Herminio joined the army to support the family. The only thing, that kept Conchita together, was her faith. One day Conchita was praying for her son Herminio to be safe while he was at war. And one silent night Conchita heard a ship's horn from far away. She told her family that her son Herminio was on that ship coming home from the war. Herminio never told anyone when he would be back from the war. But an hour passed when Conchita heard a faint whistle not far from the house and it was indeed her son coming home. But it was impossible for Conchita to hear the ship from her home. The ship dock was one or two hours away from her house.

Herminio in the Army

My Grandmother Blanca

My grandmother Blanca Hernandez was a woman who loved life. At the early age of sixteen Blanca, met my grandfather Luciano Vazquez. She was seventeen and Luciano was thirty when they got married. Luciano already had three boys of his own; Juan, Anibal, and Rafael. In 1943, Blanca gave birth to her first child, a son they named Elliott. Then in 1945 Blanca had her second son, Edward. While Luiciano's, family was growing, he, decided to open up a small store on the first floor and rented the upstairs apartment. In 1946 Blanca gave birth to her first daughter, Blanca Enelida, who was called Nellie for short. When Nellie was little, she crawled over a hole in the floor that let her see down into the store.

While growing up, Nellie would go to the hole and call for her father, who would grab a broom and use it to send candy up through the hole for Nellie.

In 1947, Blanca gave birth to another baby girl, Elba, and although they soon realized that Elba was sickly, they didn't allow that to ruin their happiness. Then to add more happiness in 1948 their third daughter, Carmelina was born. One day, as Carmelina was getting breast feed, Luciano stood watching his wife and daughter. Luciano's eyes were "shiny" and red looking, very strange. He then walked into the bathroom and shot himself. After Luciano's shocking suicide his blood family took his three sons away from Blanca. It was very hard on Blanca; after all, she had raised them for seven years. This left Blanca with her two sons and three daughters to raise, but eight months later Blanca's three-year-old daughter Elba passed away from scarlet fever.

The story behind Luciano's tragic death was that had lost the store's money to gambling debts and did not have any way to buy merchandise for his store. I guess my grandfather assumed because he could not provide for his family, he was ashamed what people would say about him and for that sad reason he decided to kill himself. People sometimes do things without thinking or out of desperation. Clearly, they are not taking into consideration those whom they leaving behind heartbroken afterward. In the end, it seems, my grandfather did not want to face the music.

LUCIANO VAZQUEZ AROUND THE AGE 31

My Grandfather Luciano and his wife Blanca and their first child, Elliott is in her arms. Luciano also had three kids that Blanca raised for seven years Juan, Anibal, and Rafael. Meanwhile, Blanca had no choice but to close the store down and left her children with her mother Conchita to go find work. Looking for work in Puerto Rico was hard, so Blanca took the next step and went to New York City to see if she could have more luck.

The story of Conchita's kids and grandkids

Meanwhile, Blanca's kids stayed with their grandmother, Conchita. Since my mother was the oldest, she had to help her grandmother with the children and the household chores. Nellie did help her grandmother by cooking for her oldest brother Elliott, and Edward. Nellie also had to help with her baby sister Carmelina while Conchita attended to her oldest daughter Antoñia who got sick. Conchita's daughter Antoñia was very smart, especially in mathematics, she also wrote poems and learned English on her own. Antoñia one day got very sick and had a stroke which rendered her deaf and mute. She had to be taken care of from that day forward.

There were many chores to do around the house. Nellie cooked, cleaned, washed, ironed clothes, and she did the dishes. My mother was very young and always wanted to go play outside, but her grandmother had her doing the dishes all the time. So, Nellie tried to hurry up and would end up breaking the plates. Afraid that she would get in trouble, Nellie would go to the chest were her grandmother kept her fine china, and take a plate out to replace the broken one. "Now let me ask this, with so many people in the house no one noticed the difference between plates? By the time her grandmother did notice, when she looked inside the chest all her good dishes were gone. My mom told us this story millions of times, and still I laugh hard. On occasions I thought about asking my mother if her grandmother had regular dishes to use every day, and they didn't look any different than the nice china that she set out for special occasions, then why put the china in the chest? I wonder if other families have had similar situations.

A Christmas Story

When Christmas came around Conchita would bring Nellie and her brothers and sister to the midnight mass. Christmas in Puerto Rico is not much different than here but in Puerto Rico there is a day that is celebrated differently. On January six, the people celebrate the day of the Three Wise Men. The children collect hay and place a bundle under their bed, then in the morning. The hay would be replaced by a toy. It was said that the Wise Men come and feed their camels and then leave a gift as a thank you for the hay. Looking back my mother remembers how her brother and sister would get a toy doll that had stiff arms and legs. The boys would get trucks and balls. Even though Conchita didn't have much money she still always managed to get them something. To bring more money into the house, Nellie would go to the neighbors' houses and clean, and she would receive fifty cents or a dollar. Another way she would help was with her brother Edward. He would go and kill livestock, and then together they would cut the meat. Then he would go to the town plaza and sell it. It wasn't much, but it was enough to keep taking care of the family and to be happy. The house Conchita lived in and raised her children Antoñia, Sarah, Herminio, Delia, Blanca and her grandchildren Elliott, Edward, Nellie and Carmelina. The next page is a picture of the house and Antoñia and her sister Sarah all grown up.

This is the house where Antoñia and her sister Sarah all grown up and all the grandchildren grew up

In 1958, my grandmother Blanca, who, still worked in New York, met a man, Luis Andujar and a year later they were married. Blanca had two more daughter's, Rolanda and Darcie. When my Aunt Darcie was little, my mother Nellie was sixteen. That year my mother moved from Puerto Rico to New York City. She went to help her mother and Luis with her baby sister's. While in New York, my mother decided to quit the eleventh grade to take care of her sister's.

When my parents met

While my mother helped take care of her sister's, she met a boy named Carmelo Ortiz. And Carmelo happened to be from her hometown in Puerto Rico. But both of their families didn't want them together. So, my grandmother sent my mother back to Puerto Rico. After three months of begging my grandmother let her return to New York, a few months later my mother and Carmelo found each other again and this time no one was going to separate them. In 1966, my mother married my father, in her hometown in Puerto Rico. My mother was happy that her grandmother could be at her wedding. My mother was twenty years old, and my father was twenty-two-years-old. My father Carmelo loved to play in his band but what he loved more was fixing cars. In 1967, I was born, in Arecibo, Puerto Rico. My father was happy to have a; newborn daughter.

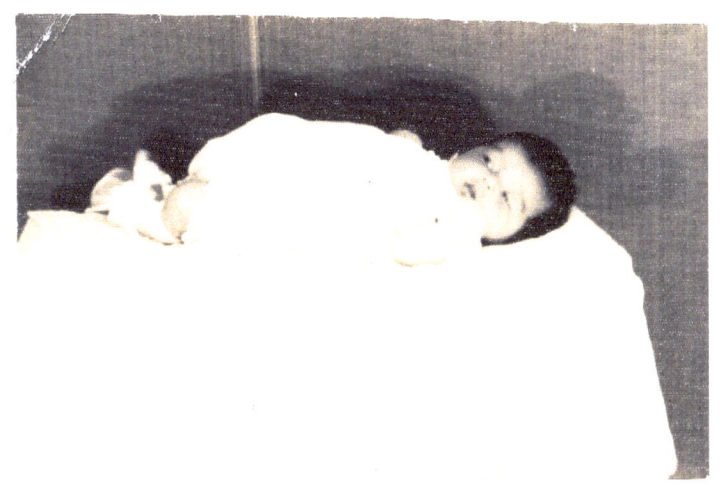

One month old

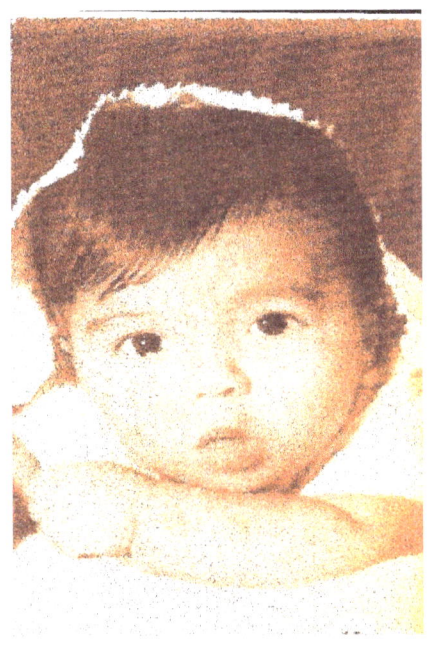

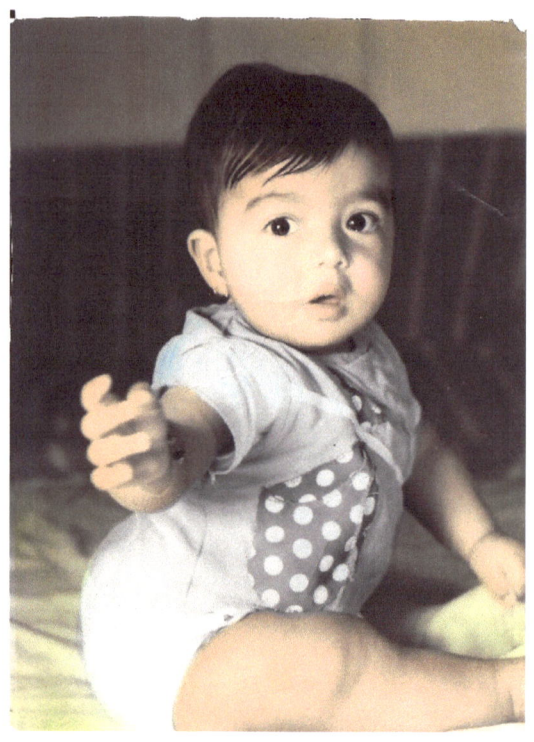

7-month-old

I guess after I was born things didn't work out between my mom and dad. My mother was devastated, but she knew she had to keep going. So, she asked her brother Edward, who now lived in the Bronx, with his wife Zaida and her daughter Connie, if she could stay with them. After a while my mother moved to her own apartment. Soon after that Edward was blessed with his second daughter Vilma.

In 1969, my father came to my mother's apartment to see me for the first time, and he wanted to give me a present for Christmas. **"SURE"** he did because the following year my brother Ferdie was born.

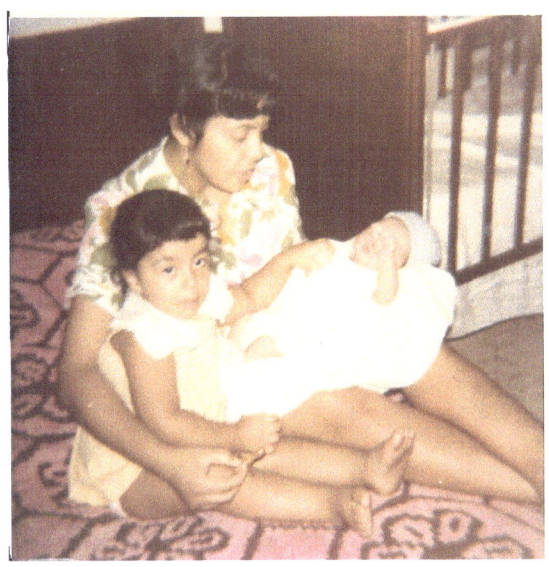

Ferdie three days old and my mother is twenty-four-years-old and me three years old.

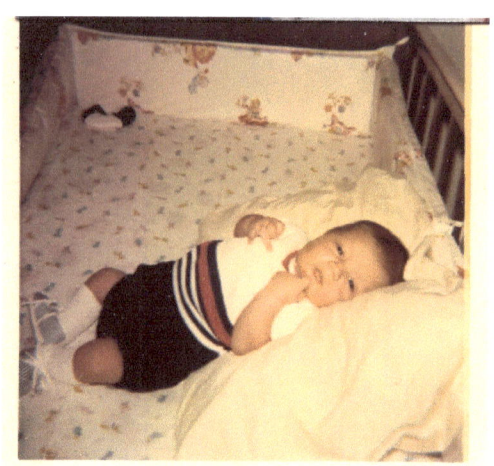

Ferdie 7 days old

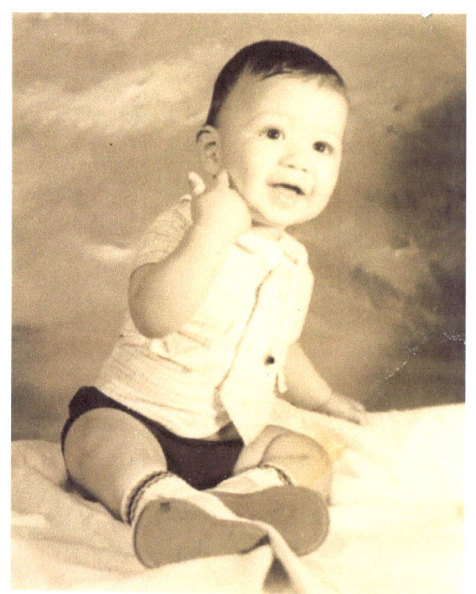

Ferdie 8-month-old

The family story

Before my, father came to visit, me he had gotten remarried to Alejandra who had a son who was born right after me. When Ferdie, was born, my father had another son. Meanwhile, my mother was planning to take us her home town Florida, Puerto Rico. So, her grandmother could meet Ferdie for the first time. My mother did not know that tragedy was heading her way, again. In 1970, before Conchita had a chance to see my brother, she had a heart attack while cooking and died. Her daughter found her on the floor. Conchita's death, was a big loss to all the grandkids. It was a great loss to lose the person who raised and care for them. Conchita was eighty-three.

My mother told us and the rest of the family what a great person Conchita was and how it meant a lot to hear her. It was fun when my Aunts and Uncles talked about the funny times when they got spanked when they did something wrong. The stories my Uncle Edward and his brother told were funny. They talked about the time my mother Nellie hid under her bed to avoid a spanking. Her brother's Elliott, and Edward went to try to get her out from under the bed. Nellie got so strong. She held on for dear life to the bottom of the bed. At the time, the bed had a box springs that were not covered, and you could see the wires. By the time, they got Nellie out from under the bed.

The wires got so stretched out they would be hanging down all the way to the floor. They laughed and laughed, talking about the good old days. I can see Conchita was a loving person who helped whomever she could.

She was also a great person to raise her children along after her husband had been murdered. And Conchita helped raise her grandkids for her daughter, Blanca. With everything Conchita had done she also had to watch her daughter Antoñia after she got sick and became deaf and mute. Conchita gave her all to her entire family. After so many years hearing my mother Nellie, talk about Conchita and hearing the stories about my great, great grandmother Conchita I wish I could have had a chance to know her.

Conchita Muñez 1890-1970   Antonia Moreda -19

The news of Eilza Muñez

My mother was raising us the best she could. In 1971 her sister Carmelina came with her daughter Blanch from Puerto Rico and moved in with us. While we all lived in the same apartment and grew up together. The conditions in the apartment were not that great. At one point, if it rained, we would need an umbrella just to use the bathroom. My Aunt Carmelina worked, and my mother stayed home and took care of us. But no matter what, they made sure we were happy. But no one knew that bad news was heading our way. In 1974, my great-great-great grandmother Eliza Muñez, passed away at the age of one hundred and fifteen. Rumors around the family were that Eliza was interviewed by a Spanish newspaper reporter from the newspaper called "El Mundo," "The World." Everything they asked her back then she answered, so they think that Eliza could've been much older than 120 years old.

Eliza Muñez was born around 1843 and passed away in 1974.

The move to Boston, Mass

We made many memories! One of the great memories was the snow storm of 1978. We were all awakened by a knock on the door. It was my Aunt Dorcie's friends Ernesto Orozco. And his brother's and sister's. They had been shoveling the sidewalk and the stairs to get to our door. There was six feet of snow covering everything, and schools were closed for two weeks. Boston had declared a State of Emergency. I remember walking with my mother and my brother Ferdie, from Dorchester to Roxbury. It took two hours for us kids and it was a blast. But from one town to the other town was at least twenty-five minute by car, and the buses and taxis were not running because of the State of Emergency.

There was so much snow that, no cars had been dug out yet and you could only see a few police cars on the street. My mother Nellie put bags from the loafs of bread under our sox also trash bag, on our feet so we didn't get our feet wet. We had fun walking to different places. I remember my mother taking us sliding in the park and whizzing down the hill. One day my mother and her cousin Laura decided to go to a friend's house that was a few minutes away by bus but twenty-minutes walking time. While we were walking, we came upon a neighborhood that had made a maze out of the snow and it looked like fun.

We decided to get up on top of the snow maze. So, while we walked on it my cousin's and my brother passed a spot where it was water covered with ice. They all passed it very easily but when I came to it, I fell down right next to it and my hands and my coat got all wet.

Everyone laughed but all I cared about was that I was freezing. A year after the storm we moved to a different neighborhood. We were the second Puerto Rican family to move there. My cousin Laura lived there for a couple of years before her and her husband moved back to Puerto Rico. Time passed and the neighbors soon realized we were quiet people, and we did not make any trouble in the neighborhood and we began to make friends.

Meanwhile, my mother Nellie provided for us as both a mother and a father. She would clean during the week so that on the weekends she could take us out to the movies or to the park. I remember my mother got my brother Ferdie and me a pair of bicycles, but we didn't know how to ride them. My mother took us to the park that was a block away from the house so she could teach us how to ride the bikes. There was one problem. My mother did not know how to ride a bike herself; she had never had a bicycle in her life. But she didn't care, she took her sister Darcie's bike and started to ride. We saw her ride straight into a basketball pole. My Aunt Darcie, my brother Ferdie, and I looked in shock, and when we went to see if she was ok, we started to laugh. The look on her face was priceless. Though she broke the reflectors on the bike, she was proud because she was showing us how to ride, and she learned a little how to ride, too. I want to dedicate the next pages to my mother Nellie.

A dedication to my mother

I dedicate this page to my mother Nellie for all the support you have given me grown up. You stopped your life to raise us and you tried your best to give us as much as you could. You raised me to become a woman that you can be proud of and be seen in a positive way. You are my mother and father both in one and that's a big honor. You've been there for us when we were sick or sad. Also, to be a woman can do anything that life has to offer.

Even if it was good or bad, you taught me growing up that anything goes even learning from our mistakes. Also, if anything goes wrong that I should leave everything in God's hands. Whatever happened you always told us that God had our back. I want to say from the bottom of my heart how much I admired you. I want to thank you, also want to thank Jesus, for choosing you to be my mother.

Mom, thank you for always believing in me. "GOD BLESS YOU." Mom, I love you with all my heart. I can't express how happy I am. and I'm so proud to be your daughter. You have done so much for us I can't thank you enough. I am so proud of you, Mom. I am honored to be your daughter. Thanks, Mom, for everything.
here.

My mother Blanca E Vazquez
At the age sixty-three
GOD BLESS YOU ALWAYS
Picture was taken in 2004

While growing up

Growing up, my mother sometimes took us for the summer to New York City to see her sister Carmelina and her husband Adrain. My brother Ferdie and I spent time with my cousin Blanch and her brother's Andy and Edwardo. While having a great time visiting my cousin's, I also got to see my other cousin's Connie and Vilma. Also, my mother Nellie took us on vacation to Puerto Rico to see my grandmother Blanca and my grandfather Luis.

We got to see my grandmother's side of the family, like her sister Delia. While visiting them, my father came to see my brother Ferdie, and I and we also had a chance to see my brother Juan, Cesar and Angel. We had fun together but it was too short a vacation. When it was time to go, it was hard on my mother to say goodbye to her mother Blanca. When we went back home and time passed my brother Ferdie, and I started school and began making friend's in the neighborhood. My brother Ferdie met his best friend's Lawrence Almeida and Matthew. As I got to know them, I also made lots friends of my own. The summer of 1983 while I was playing ball in front of the house, I remember my friend Holly's sister, little Morgan, came over to talk. Morgan told me she could not wait to start middle school. As we talked, she told me she had her new clothes that her mom got for her to start school that year.

We were talking for a while, and I remember her telling me, "I'll see you Thursday and Friday." I told her okay, I'll see you." Morgan left but as the day went by, I remember the family sat down to watch the Red Sox game that night.

The next morning, I woke up to the phone ringing and when I went to get it, I realized it was my Aunt Darcie calling. My Aunt Darcie asked me Morgan's last name. When I told her, my aunt told me that she just saw the morning news on TV. It reported that Morgan was dead. I stood frozen hearing this news. A little girl who slept in my house, who I hung out with her older sister. I couldn't believe it. I found out later that day they found her body at the park. I remembered she said she would see me Thursday and Friday; those were the days of her funeral and burial. I never understood the meaning of Thursday and Friday until I was much older; then I realized that it was strange to mention those two days.

Was I getting spiritual stuff back then without me knowing what was to going to happen in my future? I will never know. I guess I let that one go, I guess I don't want to know. As time marched, on my friends and I started to go our separate ways. We started to grow up, and we all went to different schools.

My time in high school

I started going to high school. I was a quiet person and didn't hang out in the hallways at school but went straight to my classes. At the time I didn't have friends at all. I was a shy person one day in tenth grade I was in my biology class, I was sixteen at the time, and I remember the gym teacher walked into the biology class and she asked if any of the girls wanted to play sports. I had never played sports and so I decided to stand up and said that I'd like to play softball. I did not realize that next to me was a girl named Deborah McCall. I heard Deborah say, while, touching my shoulder, that we could be on the same team. Later that day after school we went to practice but I did not know that an old classmate of mine, Susan Alexis, was also on the team. And by the time softball was over I had two great friends, actually best friends. Wherever one of us was the other was right behind. We would hang out at each other's houses almost all the time. We became best friends

This is me   Susan Alexis   Deborah McCall

The summer 1985 was around the corner. Debbie, Susan and I started to work summer jobs. I remember one summer I worked at Blue Cross Blue Shield while Debbie worked in the same building but a different department. My mother and my brother wanted to go to Puerto Rico but I could not go, I was working. So, my mother asked Debbie's mother if I could stay at her house until she came back. While in Puerto Rico, Ferdie saw our father after so many years not knowing about him. When Ferdie called me and said, I got a something to tell you. I asked him what's going on, and he said we now had a baby sister. I was so happy. I asked my brother Ferdie her name. He told me Diana, and she is two years old. When I hung up the phone, I told Debbie and everyone that I had a baby sister, and she was two-years-old. When my mother came back from Puerto Rico, my brother Ferdie gave me some pictures of my brothers Juan, Cesar, Angel and my baby sister Diana.

After I finished the summer job at Blue Cross Blue Shield, I remember that August 1985 my brother Cesar came for a visit for the first time. It was fun for me to have two brothers under one roof. I had a blast. My mother took us to show Boston to Cesar. I learned what kind of stuff Cesar liked. It was a blast watching him see new and different things. When the summer was over, and he went home the entire family missed him. Every time we saw an eighteen-wheeler we said if "Cesar was here to see it." Then summer was over and school started. Debbie, Susan and I knew that year would be different, it was going to be our last year of high school. I look back and remember we did the same thing every day. If one of us got to school early, we waited in the hallway next to a cement bench where everyone used to meet.

We were the three musketeers Susan, Debbie, and I were always together. It was a blast. Then we knew we had to save up for our prom, and we knew the senior trip was going to be great as we were going to go to Freeport in the Bahamas. The year was almost over, I remember rumors were spreading that the school wanted to change the name. Someone decided to spread the word for everyone to do a walk out and headed to downtown Boston to fight to keep the school name Madison Park High. We did the walk, something I would never forget. When it was time to go on the senior trip, we all went to the Bahamas. It was so much fun for all the kids. We went to the club, we rented scooters. Susan and I got to share a scooter.

I have to say because the wind was hurting my eyes, I closed them and I didn't see Susan was heading into some rocks. We went over the rocks and I scratched my elbow. It was funny because earlier that day Debbie and Susan were sharing the scooter while I was in front of them. I happened to lose my balance on the dirt road. I did make sure I would not fall, I decided to lean to the left side and put down the scooter down to the side. The next thing I saw was Susan and Debbie fly over my scooter and land not far from me. I could not stop laughing that day. I would never forget that good memory. Our vacation came to an end and in 1986, we graduated high school we headed out into the real world. Susan went off to college; Debbie went to work in a law firm office, and I started to work in a State Street bank for a short time. After I got laid off from the State Street bank, I decided to go to Puerto Rico with my brother Ferdie. We went to my father's house for the first time to meet my baby sister Diana who was now three-years-old.

I was having a great time spending time with my sister and brother's but because I was used to my own neighborhood, I got homesick. I was in Puerto Rico for a month. It was the longest month of my life and I felt that the time was going too slow. I felt like the hours were dragging and the weather was so hot for me. Through it all, I did have a great time with my brothers and sister. My cousin Marisa and my brother Cesar and my sister went to old San Juan, and we entered the Fortress that is called El Moro. While there I remember it started to rain. I remember my sister Diana started jumping in a puddle, so I joined in, and began jumping with her. Then a week before going back home my father rented a scooter for us to ride. While riding the scooter we were having fun. My brother's Ferdie, Juan, Cesar and I we were having a great time. I was on the back saying "beep, beep" a few times. After that my brother Cesar caught up with Ferdie and said I think something's wrong with Jennie. Juan was on the front riding the scooter. As soon as they all stopped and waited for me to catch up with them, I asked why they stopped. They asked me if I needed to go to the bathroom. I said, "No, why?" Ferdie said, "Then way is it you screaming beep-beep?" I answered, "I was saying beep, beep because my horn was not working, and I wanted to make sure people saw me coming." Thinking about it now I laugh out loud when Ferdie and I remember that day. We laugh so hard. The month of August ended and Ferdie, and I went back home to Dorchester, Mass.

My time in Bangor, Maine

I started to look for a job in 1989, with no success. I decided to go to Job Corps in Bangor, Maine. When I got there and saw where I was I felt lost within these deep woods. I was city girl. I didn't even know anyone there and was supposed to get picked up by the school bus. While I was waiting in the Greyhound bus terminal, I looked around. It was a small terminal compared to the one in downtown Boston. When the bus picked me up, we headed to one of the dorms called Bell Dorm. That's where all the new girls or guys went.

They had another much larger dorm for the other girls and guys who had been there a longer time. While I was in the Bell Dorm, I never forgot I looked around, and the only thing I saw was trees. I called my mother and told her I did not like it. My mom told me stay a little longer and see how you like it, I said okay. Then in 1990 my mother moved from Dorchester, Massachusetts to New Hampshire. I decided to go and visit her in New Hampshire. I saw it was different from Massachusetts, and after the visit was over I went back to the dorm in Bangor. While I stayed in the Bell Dorm for about a month new kids kept arriving.

I got to know each girl and each boy who stayed at the dorm after a week or two, and they keep getting transferred to the other dorm. Finally, I was transferred to the other dorm, too. While getting used to the other dorm and getting to know the girls and guys, one day my brother Ferdie called me and told me that he got a call that my baby sister Diana. She was upset that it was big sister day in her school, and she wanted me to be there with her.

I felt so bad I went back to my room and my tears came out because at that moment I realized that my sister needed me and I couldn't be there for her. At that moment I made a promise to myself that I'd try to make it to her graduation. Meanwhile, in Job Corps I studied computers, Business, file clerk and data entry. I do remember getting different roommates, but mostly I remember that all the kids ate and slept in the same building twenty-four seven. And you do become very close to each other. The dorm monitor gave some passes to the girls and guys. It was a "Class A Pass." With that Class, A Pass we could stay up late until one in the morning, and you can go off campus after school.

Now if you got written up doing something wrong, the Class A Pass would be taken away. I have to say I was too quiet or too shy to do anything so I never got my Class "A" Pass taken away. The girls and guys I got to be friends with were from all over: New York, Rhode Island, Connecticut, Maine, and some of my friends were from Fitchburg, Mass. As the months went, I began to see my closest friends start to go back to their home towns. I felt hurt, not because they left because I missed them. We were so close to each other; I even did a baby shower for one of the girls that I was close to. I remember she had a boy after she left Job Corps. While I continued meeting new kids, after a while I decided to get a job.

While I was in Job Corps when it was time to go back to the dorm sometimes at night, I started to walk around with a rock in both of my hands. The reason for that was I was a fanatic of scary movies so I thought Jason from Friday the 13th or Freddy Krueger would jump out of the woods and get me.

In 1991, my time in Job Corps ended but instead of going back home I soon realized I started to like Bangor, Maine so I decided to get an apartment there. I liked it there, but I did not stay there long. A few months later I moved to Portland, Maine for six more months. Soon my roommates in Portland, decided to move out, so I decided to go home to my mother in New Hampshire.

The start of the unknown spiritual path

My brother Ferdie, still hung around with his best friends from the old neighborhood, Lawrence and Matthew, and Lawrence's sister Marie and Ferdie started to date off and on for a while. After I came to stay with my mother, I soon realized that I liked New Hampshire, too. It reminded me of Bangor, quiet and clean, but it didn't have a lot of trees like Bangor did. New Hampshire is a nice place even though I did not have a friend in New Hampshire; they all were back in Dorchester, Mass.

I never thought moving to New Hampshire would change my life forever. One summer night in 1995 my Aunt Darcie called me to ask me if I could babysit her son Sergio. I said yes. Sergio was also my godchild; my Aunt Darcie ask me if I could come around four thirty in the morning. That way she could get to work in time. I told her it was fine with me. I got up and got dressed and started to drive to Amherst Street. It was a nice August summer night, warm, but as I kept driving, I started to notice something. I was looking at the moon and it was different. As I drove closer to my Aunt Darcie's house, I could see the moon getting bigger. But the problem was the moon was on the ground! I didn't know what to think. I started to look around to the other cars to see if the people were talking about the moon or pointing to it.

As I looked at the moon it was so bright, so round and as I kept looking, I could see the outline of it all from the inside of the moon. For me, I know the moon is supposed to be seen from the sky not from the ground.

I turned on the car radio to see if they were talking about the moon. I didn't know if it was normal to see the moon on the ground. I didn't know if it were normal or paranormal and I was shocked. I didn't know, but I kept looking for answers. I got to my Aunt Darcie's house and waited for her to go, I turned on the television so that I wouldn't miss the news report about the moon. I watched the news for a whole week, I even got the newspaper to see if I there was anything about the moon. Soon after that my mother moved back to Massachusetts. I moved in for a short time with my Aunt Darcie so that way I could take care of my godson. While she worked and during the weekend, I had a table at the flea market.

That was open at the time in New Hampshire. I loved selling toys, T-shirts, whatever I could get my hands on. I love business. I started to know the people who came to the flea market who I met each weekend. It reminded me when I was back in Job Corp when people came up to me to talk about their problem's. I just tried my best to help them out as much as I could. I would sometimes tell that person it will work out or give it time and in the end. The outcome will be surprising. I helped or gave advice too. It came out the way I said it would. **"GOOD FOR ME"** I guess even though I was surprised that everyone's outcome was ok. Were angels preparing me for the future without my knowledge?

Meanwhile, my brother's friend Lawrence and his sister Marie were Mr. James and Mrs. Charlotte Braderick's only grandkids. Lawrence and Marie loved spending time with them. As Mr. and Mrs. Braderick's got older, Lawrence's mother Joan soon realized that she needed to care for her parents. I knew Marie since she was five years old. I had always heard that their grandparents' house was haunted.

I got to know her grandfather, Mr. James and his wife Mrs. Charlotte. One day I decided to stay over their house for the first time in my life. And that night Mr. Braderick passed away. It was a terrible loss for the family. That night something happened before Mr. Braderick went to the hospital. The family dog started to howl. The problem was the only one who heard the dog howl was me, and I always heard that when a dog howls like that something bad is going to happen. The night went on and we came back home from the hospital. Maria and I were playing the Nintendo in her bedroom on the third floor. When we heard the phone ring, I told Maria to pick up the phone.

I don't like the ringing. Not knowing why, I said that we all knew the house phone sounded the same. Maria went to answer the phone and when she came back in the room she was crying; the hospital had called. Mr. Braderick had died that night. My question is why was I the only one who heard the dog howl if everyone was next to me? No one heard the dog howl and since all the house phones back in the day sound the same, I felt uneasy with the ringing. I guess I was feeling the paranormal that night. did I have the gift back then but I guess I need to look for more answers. In 1993, my brother Ferdie and Marie got married. They decided to stay in the third floor of Marie's grandmother's house and help his mother in law with her own mother. Soon afterward they realized that Marie was pregnant. In 1994, Marie gave my brother a son, Kyle. Soon Kyle came home from the hospital, and his great-grandmother Charlotte also enjoyed his company. After my nephew Kyle was born, I soon realized that I had lost contact for so many years with my father and my brothers and sister.

So, I wrote to my sister, and I found out that two of my brothers had kids. Juan had a son named Kyle, who was only a couple of months apart from Ferdie's son Kyle and my brother Cesar had a boy, Christian. I started to write back and forth with my sister Diana. I enjoyed hearing from her and my brothers. While my brother Ferdie was happy being a father and I was also happy being an aunt and Joan was happy being a grandmother, the happiness did not last long. Marie's grandmother passed away in 1995. As time went on and that pain healed, we all decided to help with the big house that my mother Nellie and I decided to move into. And Marie's mother Joan was living on the first floor in six room.

My mother and I moved to the second floor, also six more rooms. Ferdie and Marie had the third floor, which had four rooms. Rumors had it that the house was once owned by a movie star. In the old days of silent movies, the house had a bell built into the wall to summon the butler to come down from the third floor. While my mother and I settled into the second floor, I knew growing up I had heard rumors that the house was haunted and I never thought it was true. I just thought that it was a rumor.

I did love the house. It was very big I walked around the whole house, even the basement. In the summer of 1995, everything changed. One day I went to Ferdie and Marie's bedroom while they were at work to play solitaire on the computer. While playing the game, something strange happened. I heard three **"KNOCKS"** one after the other. I thought right off it was my nephew Kyle, and I shouted, "Come in," but Kyle did not open the door. Not thinking anything about it I kept playing solitaire. A few second later I heard three more knockings, again a few minutes apart. I shouted, "Kyle, come on in."

He did not come in, so I thought he could not open the door. I got up and opened the door. To my surprise no one was there. I went to the other room thinking Kyle wanted to play and he went to hide. I looked in the bathroom. I looked in the living room. I looked in the other bedroom and no one was around but I thought maybe he went back downstairs. I was not thinking back then at the time while this was happening to me. Now looking back, Kyle was only two years old, he could not have gone down the stairs so fast since he had just started to walk. Meanwhile, I went back to playing the computer. While I was playing the game solitaire a few minutes went by when once again I heard the three "KNOCKS." I soon realized where it was coming from. I turned around at that moment and I heard the knock.

It was the closet door. Chills ran down my spine. I knew no one was home. Everyone was working except my mother who was on the second floor. At that very moment, when I realized where the knocking was coming from, my mother shouted out for me to go downstairs for lunch. I ran as fast as I could, but I did not go back to my brother's bedroom unless Ferdie or his wife Marie were there. In 1997 one summer night the door to my bedroom opened. I was watching television, and I looked to see who it was but no one was there. I got up and looked in the hallway, and I did not see anyone. I went straight toward my mother's bedroom to see if she was the one who came to my room, but to my surprise she was in bed watching television. I asked her if she had happened to open the door to my room. My mother said no. I happen to go to the living room. Family friend Dino was there.

I asked him as well. Dino too was watching TV. He looked at me and said, "Why would I go to your room and open the door and not say anything? I was puzzled. That night while life continued our life changed again. Ferdie announced that Marie was pregnant and in 1996 Marie gave birth to her second child Dede. Everyone was over joyed at the news. While celebrating the birth of Dede, I was happy been an aunt again. Mean-while, strange things continued to happen around me. While the family was getting bigger, and remained very close knit, something was about to rock us all that would change our family forever.

Mental illness struck our family

My family was not aware of all the different types of mental illnesses there were until 1997, when my cousin Andy was diagnosed with Schizophrenia. It was so hard for us to understand what was going on with him. While we did not understand what was happening. it was hard to see him go through so much emotion that we did not understand. He even got sick with fever. He got amnesia and didn't know who his family was. We tried everything to bring him back, to remember us. All the cousins, aunts and uncles came to talk to him. We got so worried, but he did come around from it. Two weeks later he started to remember who we were. We were so concerned about his health. He got even worse thinking people were talking about him, but with all that drama he got so close to me. My cousin began staying with us but in a house with 13 rooms the only phone that he wanted to use was in my room.

I could not sleep at night because he slept through the day. And when it was time for me to go to sleep, he got up and wanted to talk to me. That was very hard for me to handle. At one point he walked in my room one night to talk, but I was asleep. I woke up with him standing over me. When I asked him what he wanted he said he was watching TV. The problem with that was the TV was off so I got up to talk to him, but he got up and left the room. It was hard to watch him go through this crisis so much that three to four times or more we called for an ambulance. Because he refused to eat thinking that someone was going to poison him, he even kept repeating everything over and over that people were after him.

While his mom tried to find help, we soon realized that Schizophrenia was a bad illness. But it was hard to find help if you don't have money or don't know where to find the help for this kind of illness. Our family didn't know or was not aware of this type of mental illness, and it did change our lives forever. The reason I write about my cousin's mental illness is because there are people out there who need help who might not know they have this illness. And I need to make the point of seeking treatment can help some people live a normal life.

While we were dealing with Andy's illness we noticed every time we sent him to the hospital to get help, he only stayed one or two weeks. The family was puzzled. Why would they let him go so fast if he needed help? I guess my aunt didn't have the money for a better hospital. And I believe this is the case with other family members that struggled with this illness and tried their best to understand and help that some of these good-hearted people can wind up in the street lost too. I wish all the blessing in the world to them. And my cousin is still struggling with his illness. I just want to let Andy know he is always on my mind and in my heart, God bless you and I love you always. While life went on. I found myself once again in my bedroom watching TV.

My light was off and the only light in my room was my TV. When I saw my door open, I looked to see who it was but once again was nobody there. I went straight to my mother's bedroom and asked her if she opened the door. It was kind of hard for my mother to open my door and run to her bed because her room, and my room were apart. It had a bookcase that held over five thousand books.

While I was asking my mother, "Who opened my bedroom door" our family friend, who also watching TV in the living room, overheard me and he said it was the wind that blew the door open. I looked at him and said, "You are telling me that with all the windows closed a wind will come through and open the door?" He tried to explain that one of the doors was open. That the wind came through there and again, I explained to him; we are on the second floor and the door to the main entrance had a window that was stained glass that did not open. And the bathroom that was next to my bedroom did not have a window. The little kitchen was too small and because it was winter the window was not open now.

How would a gust of wind come up from the back way if the door to the back was always closed unless we came up from the back room? He looked at me while was I telling him, I said, "Besides, how could a door to my bedroom not make any noise when you're opening beside it. It's always been hard to open." After I finished explaining to Dino, I went downstairs to the main kitchen. When I walked into the kitchen, I found my brother's mother in-law, Joan sitting at the kitchen table. She saw that I looked troubled and she asked me what was wrong. I explained to her that someone keeps opening the door to my bedroom. She advised that the bedroom that I was sleeping in was her father James Broderick's and then she said that his ghost was not going to hurt me. I looked at her and said. "Thank you, Joan for not scaring me." A month went by, and something happened that was a shock to me and everyone around me.

The death of my best friend

In April of 1997 while I was sleeping, I got woken up by a family friend, Jay, and he told me I had a visitor downstairs. When I went downstairs, I did not get to the bottom floor when I saw Lisa. She was standing by the door. I knew at that very moment that something was wrong. Lisa hardly ever visited me I hung out more with her sister Priscilla Oliver. I remembered not even saying hello, I just said to her, "What's wrong, what's going on?" Lisa looked at me and announced that my best friend of fifteen year's Deborah McCall, passed away in her sleep the night before of heart failure. I remembered running back upstairs and starting to cry. I went to my mother's room to tell her that Debbie passed away. I remember the only thing my mother said was, "Oh my God, poor Liz." Eight months before Liz McCall had lost her other child Willie McCall, also of heart problems. Willie was just thirty-one years old when he passed away. I got dressed and headed to Miss McCall's house. News spread about Debbie's death. In my family everyone knew her. I called my brother Ferdie and told him what happened. Debbie had a great heart and everyone she met loved her. I lost my best friend that year, and she was only twenty-nine years old.

Deborah McCall

March 18, 1968 -April 16, 1997

To lose a best friend was hard but I could not have imagined seeing a loving lady like Liz McCall lose not one child, which was tragic enough, but lose two within eight months' period was hard enough. I never forgot Debbie. I still see her in my sleep and I enjoy my dreams when I'm with her. Thank you, Debbie, for visiting me, even though I know it is just in my dreams you will always be in my heart. As time passed on one day I was talking to Marie in her bedroom, and I knew that she also had the gift of seeing spirits too.

When Marie felt something around her, she got so panicked that she even scared the person next to her never mind the spirit scaring you. One day I was talking to her when Marie asked me if I felt the coldness around her as I reached out to where she was, I feeling the cold. I did feel the cold but did not say yes because of the way Marie was acting, so I picked up my nephew Kyle who was next to me and left the bedroom.

In 1998, my brother Ferdie bought a two-family house in New Hampshire. While Ferdie's mother in law Joan sold the house and moved to Brockton, Massachusetts for a short time. My mother and I moved next door to my brother Ferdie's two family houses. While my mother and I settled in our new apartment a month later, public housing called and told me that they were ready to show me an apartment. I thought I would never be called because I had I waited for about a year and a half since I signed the paper. The day came to show me the apartment. When I walked into the apartment and saw the bedroom, then I went to the kitchen and then the living room, I loved the apartment. It had a view that was amazing. You were able to see the whole town from where I was standing. In September of 1998 I moved into my apartment, and I loved it. I loved watching television and no one coming to change it or play with my computer, and no one telling me to get off if it. I could use it any time I wanted to. I know I'm older but that's how I felt. While time passed and life was changing once again my family came together.

Family comes together once again

A few months went by, and bad news once again was headed our way. Our cousin Helen Hernandez took her daughter Adianez Gonzalez to a doctor's appointment. The doctor soon realized that Adianez had a bump next to her neck. When the results came in, my cousin, Helen found out that her daughter had cancer. It was a big blow. Soon we all found out what was happening. The word "Cancer" for us was big scary word, especially for the younger kids. And not knowing anyone who had cancer we stood on the sidelines watching and praying and hoping for the best. Even if we were so scared of her diagnosis.

Now a few months later in 2000 we celebrated that my cousin Adianez was cured. Adianez was a very brave person. She never gave up, and she kept going to school while she was in treatment. We felt a great joy when she was pronounced cancer free. We all celebrated. That same year my mother, my brother Ferdie and his wife Marie and I were all going on a vacation to my mother's home town Florida, Puerto Rico to visit my grandmother Blanca and the rest of the family. As I stepped into my grandmother's house, I made a quick phone call to tell my sister Diana and told her that Ferdie and I were in town. It was the greatest time to see my sister and brother's again after so many years had passed. I looked around and saw my baby sister Diana. How tall she had gotten. As I enjoyed being around my brother's, I sat back and watched and looked at everyone who was around me. I watched my brother Caesar talking to my brother Ferdie and to see my brother Juan laughing and watching his son Kyle and nephew Kyle playing and drawing on the floor.

I kept looking at my little brother Angel trying to talk in English to his sister in law Marie. Then I soon realized that not only was Marie my sister in law but I had three more sisters in laws that I needed get to know better. As we enjoyed each other's company for the first time been all grown up, it was fun to see each other again. I still had a promise to keep to myself to be there for my sister's "graduation." I never told anyone that I was keeping this promise. While time was standing still for those few moment's I enjoyed playing with all five nieces and nephews I had at the time. Soon the vacation was over, and we went back to New Hampshire. As time went on I heard that my brother Caesar and his wife Yamir Mendez celebrated the birth of their first child Sergio.

A few months went by when my brother Ferdie and his wife Marie celebrated their third child Brad that same year. The New Year of 2000 arrived; I kept my promise to myself. I did go back to Puerto Rico to see my sister Diana graduate. I was so happy I realized that I indeed kept my promise. That month of May I saw my father Carmelo for the first time. Over seventeen years had passed since the last time I saw him or heard from him. I did enjoy every minute I had with my sister. I remember she was on stage dancing to the music she was performing on her graduation. Later that day someone asked me if I was going to the prom with Diana, and I looked at them weirdly; it was not the way they asked me it was because why would I go to the prom? learned that proms in Puerto Rico are different from back home. I found out even the parents go to the prom if they want to. Not to watch the kids at the prom, the parents went to watch big music stars sing at the prom. Now for me I remember my prom.

I had a limo and a DJ but I got a senior trip that was nothing compared to Puerto Rico. I spent time with my sister those two weeks and it was great. I got to know a little more about my sister and I got to know her mom Alejandra. I even got a chance to see my brother Cesar and his wife Yamir's new son Sergio and spent time with my brother Angel and his wife Elizabeth as well my brother Juan and his wife Stacy. My time in Puerto Rico came to an end and when I got back to New Hampshire. I made sure I called my step-mother Alejandra to let her knew I'd arrived home safely and to thank her for everything. Coming home was great but little did I know that what was about to happen to me would change my life forever.

When my life started to change

It was a regular hot summer evening in August of 2000; it was a day like every other day. I was in my apartment and on the computer, and I got tired and went off to bed. Like every night before going to bed I prayed, and I dozed off around two-twenty in the morning. I was awakened by someone "jumping" on my bed. When I opened my eyes to the feeling of someone still "jumping" on my bed, I started to pray asking Jesus to help me. As scared as I was, I calmed myself down and turned over and fell asleep. Once again while totally asleep. I saw a teddy bear coming toward me and I opened my eyes, and shouted asking Jesus to help me. I was scared. I started to pray the Hail Mary and stayed up for a few seconds more when I decided to turn over and go back to sleep. I dozed off again. When I heard a loud "THUMP" I sat up to see where the noise came from. I never imagined in my life what was about to happen. I turned toward the door where the thump came from and as I turned to look at my bedroom door I quickly got up.

I was shocked by what I saw. I was looking at a little boy walking away and "VANISHING" into thin air. I was so scared I jumped off my bed and ran to the phone. I called my mother and told her I had just seen a ghost. At two-thirty in the morning I left my apartment crying and I drove to my mother's house. When I got there, my mother saw how scared I was, and she tried to calm me down. She asked me to tell her what happened so while she was trying not to cry herself being the nervous person she is, I began to tell her what had happened, and she was shocked by what I was telling her. I remembered that my sister in law Marie came to my house for a visit a few days before.

I went to the second floor and went straight to my brother Ferdie's bedroom. On Marie's side of the bed I pointed my finger at Marie, "screaming" at her. "Did you see something the last time you came over?" I knew Marie was sleeping. She didn't know why I was screaming and pointing my finger at her. For that matter, she did not even know why I was crying. Marie finally opened her eyes and looked at me and the only thing that Marie said was, "What are you talking about?" Marie sat up and asked what was wrong with me. I asked her again if she had seen something in my apartment the last time she came over and she said, "No, if I did I would have told you."

Marie asked me what happened and why was I crying and pointing my finger at her? We decided to go to the living room, and we sat down. Marie asked me again, 'What happened to you?" I started to explain to her what happened from the beginning. I finished telling her that I saw the boy walking away from my bedroom and vanishing. I did ask Marie once again, "Did you see anyone in my apartment the last time you came to visit me?" Marie knew I was scared she looked at me and said, "I told you no, if I did I would have told you so." I started to tell Marie what the boy looked like. "He had a white glow around him, and he wore a white shirt and pants."

Even I could not explain why I knew it was a boy, but I felt that he was. But I didn't see his face since he walked away and vanished. But I did see his hair, it was black. Marie looked at me and said, "Now you know how I feel when I see things." I looked at her and said, "Well you have been seeing spirits since you were eleven years old, you are used to it, not me."

That night was the longest night of my life. After a while we all went back to bed I stayed in my mother's room. The next day I wanted to find out how long the building been up and what year they built it. I went back to my building, and I found Lois Stewart who lived there and I walked into the lobby and asked Lois what year the building was built. Lois looked at me and asked me what was wrong. I proceeded to tell her what happened to me that night. While I told Lois the story, she looked at me and said, "The building has been up for only thirty-five years." Meanwhile, I came across Dorothy Legere.

She also lived in the same building, and I also asked her how long had the building been up. I wanted to make sure I kept asking people. I also asked Becky, and Joyce Seyer how long the building had been up, and every one of them said thirty-five years. A lot of people in the building found out what had happened to me, that I saw a little boy, and all. I did enter my apartment, but I decided to stay over my mother's house again. Meanwhile, I kept asking my sister in law Marie if she could come to my house and see if she could feel the little boy. I knew Marie was scared of her gift and would get panicked when she felt them around her. I didn't care if she was scared. I needed to know why I saw a little boy, and I kept asking her to help me out until she finally said yes. Three days later Marie came over with me to see if she could feel the little boy. While we were in my apartment Marie asked me if I was on my bed when I saw the boy. I told her yes. Then Marie went and sat down on the edge of the bed at the headboard. Marie took a few deep breaths and waited a few minutes when she looked at me and said, "I feel him, he is here." Marie started describing him how he looked.

I kept saying, "Yes, that's how I saw him." Marie also said he looked like around eight or ten-years-old. I said yes, that I believed that based on how tall he looked like he could be that age. Marie then asked him why was he there. The little boy told Marie that he wanted to show me that; it was just the beginning for me. Also, he said he wanted to play with me and to my surprise. I said at two thirty in the morning he wanted to play? He could not wait till morning? Even though I never forgot what the boy told Marie he came to show me it was just the beginning for me.

"MAN, WAS HE RIGHT!"

When I went back home five days later, I went into my room to use the computer. When I felt a cold hand touch my back, I ran out of the front door back to my mother's house. Then I went back two days later, and I stayed in my apartment one day but I left all my lights on. I went to my mother and told her it could be the mattress that I got from my Aunt Carmelina a few weeks before. I decided to throw out the mattress and get my old bed back. I did call my Aunt Carmelina, and I explained why I threw out the mattress. I told her that I believed the mattress was haunted. By then my mother had already told her why I left my apartment in the middle of the night. After a while, everything again became almost normal. When I started to see shadows pass by my room, and I ran out of my apartment back to my mother's house. Each time I kept seeing shadows walking past my room. I kept going back and forth from my apartment to my mother's house. I did try to stay in my apartment. But one night I saw something go by me. I called my mother to come and get me and I went to wait for her in front of the building.

While I was heading out the door, I could see a bright light following me. I was impressed how the light followed me and I smiled. I don't know why I didn't get scared. I guess because I was outside, I felt safe. I keep trying to sleep in my apartment, but I was losing sleep. I catch up with my sleep when I went to my mother's house. One day I was in my apartment watching TV in my living room when the phone rang and it was my mother. While we were talking something happened to catch my eye. Even though it was day-time I could see that on the couch next to me was a shadow figure. It looked like a man sitting on the couch. I did not run but I did tell my mother what I was seeing.

Then one day I looked toward the dining room wall, and I saw an eye. I got spooked but kept quiet. I thought, man, now I am seeing thing's but then it changed position. The next time I saw it; again, it was on the living room wall. Now this time it was day time when I saw the eye and this time it had a lot of glitter with it. When I shouted, "What do you want from me?" It began to get bigger and bigger until it looked like Jesus Christ. Let me say I didn't let it finish forming. I got up from where I was sitting and ran out the door. At the same time, I said out loud, "I do believe in You and I know You are protecting me, but I am scared" and left. I started to see a lot of glitter next to the door way in my bedroom. In the following days I kept seeing a lot of glitter, but it had a glowing light with it. I could not sleep, but I could not keep running from my apartment, so I decided to ask my Uncle Edward's wife Maria if she could go with me to public housing office. The day came that my Aunt Maria went with me to housing. I asked the lady at the front desk if I could speak to someone.

The lady asked me what was it about. I did not want to lie, I guess I needed to tell the whole truth. When I looked at the lady and told her why I wanted to be moved she asked me again "why I wanted to be moved." I told her straight out that I had seen a ghost in my apartment. The lady looked at me and said, "Let me see if I can find someone for you to talk to." She stepped back to the back room no more than a second later and I heard laughter coming from the room. Then it got quiet, and the lady told me someone will be right with you. Then I sat down to talk to the lady. She asked me why I wanted to move. I did not want to lie; I looked at her and said I had a problem in my apartment and I saw a ghost there. The lady told me to sign some papers to see if they could do something to move me, but I did not hear anything from them after that.

When I left the office I went back home, I kept trying to sleep, but I felt my hair had been touched. And sometimes I felt like my hair had been touched so much that I had to go and check my hair in the mirror to see if I had a bug or something in it. I even had two pairs of earrings on and I felt them being moved and clicking each other. I tried to see if I could make the earring's click. I moved my head different ways and it did not make any sound. Then the phone started to ring and no one spoke on the other end of the line, but it kept ringing over and over. Then the lights kept blowing out in my room or the bathroom, even the kitchen light. All in one month. I knew that was not normal as time passed. I had to buy light bulb's because that was a twice a week occurrence and I know it was not normal. I even got different lamps thinking it was the lamps, but it was not. As the month went by things keep happening without any explanation.

I did not know what to do, I was not sleeping well, I still felt the little boy jumping on the bottom of my bed. I decided to go back to public housing, and I asked if they would move me. When I sat down with the same lady and told her the reason, I wanted to be moved she looked at me and said, "If you are feeling the supernatural and seeing stuff you don't think it will happen in another place? I sat there not saying a word; this lady had a point, but I did sign a paper; however, I never was moved. As day's and months went past, I got a phone call from my sister in law Mother Joan. We talked and she knew what I was going through. Joan told me that she was reading the newspaper, and she saw that there was a Psychic Fair on February 12, 2000 in Hudson, New Hampshire.

I was happy to hear that. Those two weeks were the longest two weeks in my life. I needed some answers. I was getting ready to make a "choice" that no one knew I was making. I asked Marie if she could go with me and I asked my friend Blondie if she wanted to go with me to a psychic fair. When Saturday came, I picked up Marie and my friend Blondie and while we were heading to the Psychic Fair, I had to stop by my apartment for a few seconds to get something.

I entered the lobby and Becky who lived in the same building crossed my path. Becky knew what was going on with me. When I told her that I was going to a Psychic Fair. Becky told me to ask for a lady named Jacky Joy. I looked at Becky and I asked why and she told me that Jacky Joy is a good psychic and that she does spirit writing. I looked at Becky strangely and I answered, "Spirit writing"? "What is that?" I thought psychics just do palm reading or read the cards, I never knew they could do more than that.

Becky told me make sure to ask for her, she is good. So I left, and when I got to the Psychic Fair in Hudson, New Hampshire I told Marie and Blondie what Becky had recommended. We got to see the list at the entrance of the hall to see if Jacki Joy was available to read us, and we found her name, and I asked Blondie and Marie if I could go first. When I got to Jacki Joy's table, she could see that I was almost in tears. Jacki Joy asked me what I wanted to know, and I said, "I just need to know what is going on with me." Jacki then asked me if I wanted her to read my hand or read me the cards, but I told her, "I had heard you do spirit writings. That is what I want." So, she took her pen and paper and said okay. Jacki Joy started to write everything down and the same time she looked at me and started to tell me what was happening to me. Every word she said was amazing. Jacki was telling me that what was happening to me in my house. It was angels trying to communicate with me. She kept telling me that what I was seeing and hearing was nothing to be scared of.

As the words came out of Jacky's mouth, I began to cry because I felt like a rock began lifting off my shoulders. Jacki saw how badly I was crying. She asked me why I was so scared. I said I didn't know what was happening to me, and I saw so many things at once. Now I know what's been going on. Jacki explained how angels communicate and that what I am seeing is beautiful. After Jacki finished writing, I thanked her for everything. When I walked back to Marie and Blondie's table, they saw that I was crying. Blondie went up next to see Jacki Joy mean-while Marie asked me why was I crying. "Did the lady say something bad?" I looked at Marie and said, "No, Jacki said many thing" that she would have never known and the reason I was crying was because I thinking to do something today."

I was going to tell Mom that I wanted to move back home with her, but I decided not to. When we got back to Marie's house my mother was waiting for us. Marie told my mother that I was crying. My mom asked me, "Why did the psychic said something bad?" I looked at my mother and said, "No." The psychic Jacki Joy told me what I needed to know. I explained to my mother what Jacki told me then I said the reason of my crying was because I was thinking of moving back with you, but I decided I was going to win my fear back. Well, I felt I had to win my fear back no matter what the cost. I know I kept running out of my apartment, but I would then remember what Jacki Joy said to me. Two months went by, and I needed more information. I decided to call Jacki in Milford, New Hampshire to make an appointment, and when Jacky Joy heard from me, she sounded happy.

She told me that she could not stop thinking of me, and she told a friend how she wondered how I was. While we were talking on the phone, I asked Jacki if I could make an appointment to see her. The day came when I got to see her again; I was sitting in her kitchen when she asked me what kind of reading, I wanted. I looked at her and said, "The spiritual writing." But to my surprise I did not know that psychics have different kinds of readings. Jacki told me she could do energy readings, even palm reading and the card readings. While I was curious about all the different ones, all I wanted was the spiritual writing. Jacki got ready and started to write, she told me more about the boy that is in my house. She started writing about many things. She said the little boy appeared to me the way he did because he was preparing me for how I was going to see others. and that I would be traveling across oceans on vacation.

She said that my journey was about to begin and that I was going to be hearing many voices, but my spiritual guide would be protecting me. I went home thinking that I did understand everything she told me and the answers I was looking for. I went home and sat down to read the paper with everything Jacki had told me. I never thought most of the predictions would not come true. I decided to stay in my apartment. Meanwhile, I kept going to the stores to buy light bulbs. Months kept going by and I kept running out of my apartment. My friend knew what kept happening to me. But what was about to happen next even Jacki Joy couldn't have predicted.

Seeing Auras and Sparkles

I went to my friend Hollis, and I asked her if she could tell me where there was a Spanish church. Hollis told me next to Canal Street is a church that gave Spanish masses on Sunday and is called St Francis Xavier. On January 2, 2001 I went to church with my mother. I entered the church. I was happy, it reminded me of the church where I used to go to in Dorchester, Massachusetts Saint Peter's. I walked in with my mother. I saw a lady whose name was Lourdes. At that moment my mother and I thought that Lourdes was my Aunt Carmelina's friend from Boston. As I introduced myself to her and asked her if she knew my Aunt Carmelina and her husband Adrian, she said, "Yes," but later I found out she knew two people who had the same name as my aunt and uncle. As the mass started, I sat and watched and heard the mass at the end of the mass the same person, Lourdes got up to talk about what was about to happen in church that following weeks.

Lourdes talked about the coming events, suddenly a light turned on around Lourdes. I was so focused I did not see everyone around me. I was looking to the color blue, yellow, white, green and brown. As I kept looking at those beautiful colors it was so amazing. It doesn't compare to the colors we see every day. I asked my mother if she saw what I was witnessing. She asked me what I was seeing. I explained to her it was the most beautiful and amazing colors I had ever seen. When Lourdes finished talking about the events the color vanished. I kept talking to my mother about it. When Lourdes came up to us to ask how we liked the mass, my mother told her what I just saw.

To my amazement, Lourdes looked at me and hugged me and said, "I needed that." Later I learned what I saw around Lourdes was her aura. I told my friend Hollis and her sister Blondie what happened that day. Meanwhile, I kept going to church. While things kept happening to me I kept asking my mother to come pick me up. After a while I was getting used to seeing the shadow running by my room, and I could see the light but I couldn't explain where it has come from and I could see the sparkles. I was in my room; this time it was day time. I was playing on my computer when I saw the sparkles again in the doorway going out toward the hallway.

When I saw the sparkles I shouted out, "What do you want from me?" I heard three knocks from behind me. It was at the wall next the window. I knew no one was outside my apartment because it was on the fifth floor. And it was not coming from next door because the wall to the other apartment was on the other side of the room. That is the moment I got up and ran as fast as my legs could carry me. My heart was beating fast, and I said out loud, "me and my big mouth." Well, I was getting used to seeing people's aura and got used to my hair being touched but I realized that when I felt them around.

That when my ear started to ring different, I couldn't explain it. Every time I could see the light in the doorway or feel the little boy jump on my bed, I felt a ringing sensation in my ear. I guess that when I noticed and began to realize that when I could see the spirit that when I knew they were around, by the ringing of my right ear. One night I was on my computer, but I walked away toward my bed while I was away. I looking toward my desk.

I noticed that I had my purse on top of my desk, but the strap of the purse was hanging down, and I could see the strap swinging back and forth. I kept watching it, and it continued to swing back and forth and I know for a fact that I was away from my desk and I didn't touch the strap to make it swing like that. Someone was playing with it. I stepped back toward my bed again and I noticed the light started to flicker until it went out. Then the phone would ring, no one was at the other end. And the caller ID had no number on it, and it didn't register that the phone was ringing.

Then on April 14, 2001 my life changed once again. The week before Easter, I found myself once again in my bedroom playing on the computer. When I happened to look to my right side to my bedroom door something caught my eye, and I looked towards the bedroom door. When I looked, I noticed something incredible? I could see the door to my bedroom had changed completely. It took the form of angel wings, but the most incredible thing about it was that between the wings. In the right side of the wing was the "VIRGIN MARY" "and on the left was "JESUS CHRIST'S" face.

I was without words. I went closer to look at the door, and I was shocked what I was seeing, I turn and ran to the phone, and called my mother. I told her she needed to come over to my apartment right away. That she needed to see what I just witnessed in my house. While I waited for my mother to come over my apartment, I left and I asked two of the ladies, Paula and Bertha who were in the lobby if they both could come to my apartment to see something that I just happened to see. While Paula knew about me, and had seen, the boy vanishing, for Bertha was the first time. I had just met her that day.

We went back upstairs to my apartment, and I showed Bertha and Paula and asked them if they saw what's at the door. I remember Bertha and Paula looking at the door and then they looked at one another and Paula looked at me and said, "I see, "Jesus Christ's face." Bertha put her hand on her mouth and said, "Oh my God. I see Jesus' face. They both pointed at the door and pointed out the wings. I remember Bertha was so amazed by what she saw she said to me, "Thank you," and hugged me. As both of them were going out the door, my mother rang the buzzer. When my mother got to the fifth floor and she saw me waiting at the door for her, she asked me what the emergency was. I looked at her and said, "You need to see this." I walked her to my bedroom and asked her, "What you see in my door?

She stepped back and shouted, "Oh my God, I see the Virgin Mary!" and went directly toward the door and said, "I can see the face of Jesus." While my mother stood looking at the door, she did not have any words to say. I called my friends Blondie and her sister Hollis to tell them what was happening in my apartment. Everyone who knew me found out, everyone came to see my door. I showed the door to my friends. My mother called her sister Carmelina and told her about the door. When my friend Blondie and her sister Hollis came to see the door, they could not believe their eyes while Hollis son's Lalo and Jerry came to my home to witness the door.

While word spread about the door and people kept coming over. Everyone had a way of expressing them-selves including Mayra and her daughter Melissa Rodriguez and Marya's sister Maria and her other sister Iris Santiago as I remember.

They all started to hug me and were telling me I was very blessed. Mayra's other daughter Katiria Montero asked me how I noticed the door change. I told her that I was playing on the computer but something caught my eye and when I looked, I was shocked to see Jesus Christ and the Virgin Mary. While each person touched the door, some people touched me; I did not understand why, some people asked me to touch them, but it was indeed a miracle to see the door how it was shaped. Everyone kept talking about the door. Edelmira Rivera Mayra's mom was over, and I noticed that she was kneeling down next to my bed. She was crying, but I did notice her hip was hurting her, and she was limping. Edelmira came up to me when it was time to go, and she held my hand and told me thank you for taking your time to show me the door. Edelmira also said you are very blessed, but she also wanted me to touch her like everyone else that came to my apartment.

I kept showing the door and someone that came asked me how come I don't call the TV reporter or newspaper about the door. I said if someone else has not done it by now, so I guess it was not for the whole world to know about it at this moment time.

These next few pages are pictures of the bedroom door.

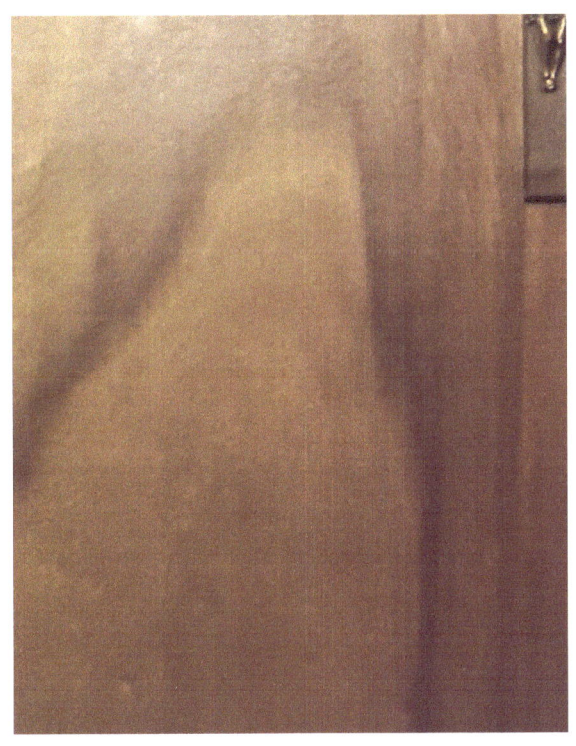

You can judge for yourself: this is the door to my bedroom.

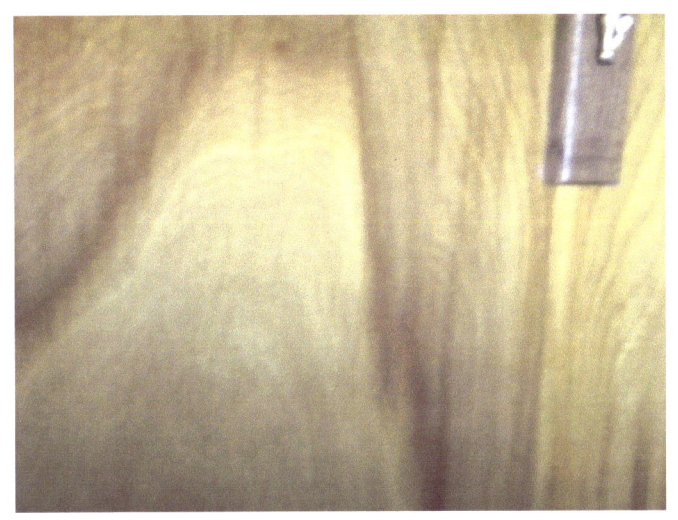

Like I said, you be the judge

I was surprised after so many years hearing about miracles and seeing TV reports of the Virgin Mary crying. And a wall outside of the church taking the form of Jesus Christ and many other images, I never thought it would happen to me. I know a lot of people can judge each time they see an image that some people see, and some people don't see it. As I sit here thinking and writing this book people will have their opinion, and I know I will get a lot of people saying different things, but I actually lived it and experienced it.

A word of wisdom
Please love one another.

The next day I had more visitors come to my home, including the Maria Anaya's family, all her son's and daughter's in law came to see the door. But later that day I went to a funeral that was one of Maria's relatives, and while I went to pay my respect to the family. I walked into the funeral home, and I found myself standing in the doorway. I was looking at everyone but at that moment Edelmira came up to me and said, "Jennie, look at my legs, it doesn't hurt anymore. I can walk fine." I laughed, and she said it is not funny. I responded by saying I don't know why I just find it strange what is happening around me.

What I didn't know was I found out later that Edelmira's legs were hurting her for over a month, and I have no explanation why it didn't hurt her any-more. After I spoke to Edelmira I continue inside to pay my respects to the family. That was when the priest started to pray and at that very moment, I felt like I had a need to look toward the wall. When I did, I could see an image appearing; what I saw was a lady with a skirt but behind her I could see the gate of heaven. I could not see the lady's face. When the priest finished talking, I walked away and as I did my friend Hollis noticed that I was looking at something because she walked up to me and asked me what was wrong, did I see something? I looked at Hollis and told her I just saw the gate of heaven, and I could see a lady in a skirt waiting but I did not know who it was.

Hollis looked surprised and responded by telling me; that was the relative" mother waiting for him. I did not know at the time until that moment his mother was dead. A few days later as I was walking to the elevator, I saw Bertha, and we talked. Bertha told me that after she had left my apartment, she felt something different and that she felt hopeful because she was waiting for the results of some blood work to see if she had cancer. I remember to my surprise Bertha said, "As you touched me, I had a feeling that I was very blessed."

I looked at her in total shock from what she was telling me when she told me her cancer was in remission it was gone. I looked at Bertha with amazement. I then said, "Thank God. Congratulation for the good news." Bertha looked at me and said to me, "You gave me faith more than you ever know." I watched Bertha walk into her apartment.

I stayed in the hallway with amazement as to what Bertha just finished telling me. That night I prayed to Jesus if He put me on this earth for a purpose then I will accept everything He wants to give me. Then one night I was on my computer talking to my friend, Blondie, we both had a video camera. And we were talking back and forth at that moment I told Blondie I see the light at the door, and it was bright and I could see something floating in the air. I was noticing that when I saw the sparkles and my ear started to ring different. While I was telling Blondie, this information, Blondie happened to be talking to her son Bob. She told him to look at me, then Blondie told her son Bob to look at what is happening around Jennie. As they both looked in the video camera Blondie told her son Bob to look at my room.

Meanwhile, I did not know that Blondie was talking to her son Bob, she never told me anything until I saw her the next day at her sister Hollis' house. We were hanging out when Blondie looked at me and said, "Look, I have to tell you something. But I did not tell you last night, I didn't want you to be running out of your house again." I asked her, "Tell me." I was curious to know what Blondie had to tell me. Blondie started to tell me, "Remember last night we were talking on the video camera?" I looked at her and responded by saying, "Yes, what about it?"

Blondie, explained that while I was telling her about my ear ringing and me seeing and feeling things going on in my bedroom, she called out her son Bob to come into her room. She told him look in my room as I looked at her strangely, and she told me they both had seen my room change color to the color blue; it was blue all around me.

I looked at Blondie so surprised and I said, "What did you see?" Blondie said while she was seeing me in the video behind me was changing to blue. It was all around me and then her son spoke out, saying that he was also there and it was true: my room turned blue. When I went back home my curiosity got to me. When I was in my room, I looked at the door, and I thought about what Blondie told me earlier that day. I decided to put the video camera facing the door and then I went to bed and went to sleep.

On May 2001, I woke up and went straight to the computer to look at the video. When I looked at what I recorded of the door. I was so shocked! What I saw on the video showed a lot of crosses and light and I could not explain where it was coming from and it kept changing colors. It looked like the sun-set, and the sun was behind a lot of crosses. I was seeing the crosses changing position. On the door, the images were so clear it was so many different faces from the other side but I could not make out who they were. While I did not finish the video, I was so shocked that I quickly got on the phone and called my mother. I told her she needed to come over to see what I'd recorded on the computer. When my mother came over and asked me now what is happening, I immediately said come into my room.

I told my mother to sit down in front of the computer and I then showed her the video. When my mother started to see the video, her mouth dropped open. She could not believe what I had captured on the video, and she kept repeating, "I see a lot of crosses, but I can see like the sunset going down and changing positions."

A day later Becky who lived in the same building came to my apartment to see the video, and that same day my friends Hollis and her sister Blondie were over and I showed all three of them the video. They kept shouting, "Look at the cross-move position, look at the color!" We watched the video for a while. Hollis said it looked like faces trying to show themselves. Our eyes were glued to the computer, and then Becky asked me if I saw the end of the video and I said, "No, not yet, I've been busy seeing the beginning of the video."

At that moment, they said fast forward to see what we see each time; I fast forwarded we saw more crosses and images of the light. Then as I kept forwarding, when we got almost to the end of the video I looked and pointed and shouted, "You see what I see?" All of us saw the angel pop out of the corner of the door. Becky, Hollis and Blondie shouted back, "Oh my God, look at that, yes, it's an angel!" As we kept looking the angel looked like it was playing the game peek-a-boo. As the video finished, the angel vanished and we looked at each other in amazement. I kept watching the video by myself. I tried to save the video.

But somehow the computer froze, and I lost the clip of the video. I could not believe that I lost the video. I did not try to put the camera to record again, but I did once in a while keep putting the camera to watch different colors of light, blue, yellow and white. Once in a while I did go back and record with the camera to check if I could see something different. To see if the light would keep showing be up differently: at one point, I could see a little stair and a door opening. I kept looking and I saw different images, but the crosses would keep jumping in a different spot.

May 14, 2000 my aunt Carmelina, her daughter Blanch and my cousin Leonor and her daughter Helen Hernandez and her kids Adianez and Ariel Gonzalez and Helen's niece Nylia Arce came to my apartment to see the image on the door, since my mother had been telling them what was happening. They all started to point at the door and were saying the door looked like it was in the shaped of an Angel's wing. Then my Aunt Carmelina said, "Look at the Virgin Mary, she looks like she is looking down." Aunt Carmelina and the rest of the family started to pray while I was praying. I then noticed a lot of sparkles around my bedroom. Then I saw my Aunt Carmelina started to cry inconsolably, and when we all finished praying, I told them about the video I had recorded. I explained that somehow, I could capture the images with the computer's camera. I told them about when my friends Hollis and Blondie and Becky were visiting and saw the angel pop out in the corner of the door.

I told each of them to stand in front of the door. One by one they stood in front of the door and the video captured crosses by their side. I could see their aura and then I could see the aura without the video as each person stepped in front of the camera. While each person went in front of the camera at that moment, I told my cousin Nylia to stand in front of the door. Everyone could see crosses next to her, but it was a light that got my eye. While everyone watched the computer, I was seeing the glitter all around her. And I could see the outline of a person but that was the most I could see, I could not tell who it was at the time, and then my mother told everyone to look at me. She explained that when I go and stand in front of the door every time I stand in front of the door, in the video you and could see a big white light go all around me.

With a lot of crosses around the door, my family was amazed what the door, was showing them. We all started to talk to each other about, and everyone kept telling me it is a miracle and that God is watching over me. Then everyone decided start to head home. My Aunt Carmelina turned and faced me and said, "You should not be scared, you have a beautiful thing here." I told her I know and then she left. A few weeks later my Aunt Maria and her daughter Ivonne Hernandez, also came to my apartment. My Aunt Maria told Ivonne to look at the door, and I remember Ivonne's face changed. She was shocked to see the image of Jesus.

Ivonne and I talked for a while, then the day went by fast as the family of Maria Anaya came once again to see the door with the camera. It was so amazing what we all witnessed. We all were standing and watching where the crosses will pop next. Someone said, "Have you tried the wall to see if you see something else or it will show the same." I said, "No, I have not done that." Well, I changed the camera to the wall we were blown away by what we saw. We were all surprised, each of us saw people! Each one of us screamed out loud do you see that man or woman? We didn't recognize anyone. But all we saw were people looking back at us. Then one of the guys in the room pointed out and said, "Do you see what he's got on his hand?" We all agreed it was a cup. But the next thing the man did was drink out of the cup, and they all started to laugh at us. Every time we turned to see the wall and pointing where the person was standing, we were shocked, but at the same time we were watching them they were watching us. While we keep watching them, we were shock that the cup looked like the cup the priest from the church used to drink the wine from.

That was the only time I ever put the video camera on the wall. For some reason or another I didn't get scared, and I stayed home that night. I didn't go anywhere after seeing that video with the image of those people.

When I sat down in my room and reflected on how many people came over to my house, I believe it was around one hundred people, it was a blessing I shared with family and friends. While I sit here writing about this, it is also blessing by sharing this with whomever is reading this at this very moment. While everything quieted down and everyone stopped coming to my house, I also stopped looking at the door unless I felt that, I had to.

After I had lost the video of what I captured from the door, I did try to save it. After that my computer froze and after that I lost the video and after that the camera broke. I never went out and got a new one. I could see without the camera but with the camera I have to say you could see it clearer. That was nothing to what I was going to see next would change my life forever.

Medium Reading

I still kept looking for answers, "I was still very curious." One day I heard about a medium who was in Boston, I asked my sister in law's mother Joan if her friend could get some information from the Boston medium's office. Four months later Joan called me and told me that her friend got the number where I could contact the medium. When finally, that day came I got to see Rev. Simen, is a medium in Boston. Rev. Simen, opened the door, he just asked me to take a seat, and a few seconds later he started to read me. Rev. Simen told me that I had a healing hand and that the boy needed to give me a message that the next time I saw him ask him what does he wanted. Then Rev. Simen said that I am like him. He also said that I will be helping people. He even described my mother's side of the family that passed away and my father's side of the family that passed away. He described them so well that each person I knew who they were except for one that I didn't know.

The Rev Simen said she died of cancer; it took a couple months to find out if she truly died of cancer. I did find out it was true, but I did not know her because the lady was related to my father Carmelo's side of the family, it was his aunt. I was happy with the reading and I went home understanding I was going to have the same gift that my sister in law Marie has.

BOY, WAS I WRONG!!!

One day I was in my mother's house talking to my her about what was going on in my apartment and without any warning a white feather just came down between both of us. I smiled and told my mother look at the feather. My mother smiled, I knew that she did not have a bird and no one in the house had a feathered coat. It was surprising and amazing the bird feather fall out of nowhere. While we were growing up, we always believed in angels and coming from a Catholic family, I started to go more to church as everything started to calm down, I even stopped running from my apartment. Even when they kept playing with my hair or the boy sometimes keep jumping on my bed at night, but I began to get used to it.

Even though the boy kept jumping on my bed I didn't dare ask him what is the message he wanted to give me. Even though the reverend said to ask the boy when I saw him, well, I felt him when he was around but I have not seen him like I did the first time. As the months went by, I realized that 70 percent of my dreams were coming true. That was when I started to write the dreams down and remember them very clearly. As the year went by, I started to understand that I will see things, but I kept sleeping with the light on. While I didn't forget what Jacki Joy told me or the reverend.

In May 2001, I saw my brother Ferdie doing a web-site. I asked him, how he did he do the site, and Ferdie took 15 minutes to show me how to start a website. I sat down and watched how he did it then I went home and started my website. Once I started the website I decided to write about the little boy and what I experienced in those couple of months. While I kept doing my website, I wrote about the little boy, really, I wanted to put funny stuff like I've seen in different websites.

I soon realized I needed to find a picture for it when I finally finished my website; it took me three months. What I ended up writing was religious over the two months' period, over three thousand people read it and signed it. I had to clear the names of those that signed the guest book on the website because it got too full. What is incredible about it is strangers talking in chat rooms and telling me how good the website was, and some people asked me to help them out with a prayer. I tried my best to help them out. I read what they had to say and responded to them as best I could. Some asked me if I was a medium or a psychic, I just kept telling them the truth, I didn't know what I was. I know some people ask me if the story on my site was true, I did laugh sometimes because people say oh it was scary story but I got a few that signed my guest book.

I won't say what they said, I know that was their opinion and like I said I really don't care. I tried helping out whomever I could. Then as months went by, I began to realize my site became religious with a few pages that were different, it was about myself but I tried to be funny with it. Also, to the point so many people got on it that sometimes the site went down for a while. I began to read a book from every psychic out there but one day I decided to write to each one of them to see what they could tell me? Then one day I had a dream that I kept seeing alphabets sending me each letter and one letter I could see a spelling a word that spelled light then another word saying healing.

When I woke up, I said to myself what kind of strange dream that, was but two days later I got two responses back from two psychics and when I looked at the envelope I was blown away.

In one envelope I read the word "light" and the other envelope I read the word "healing." My jaw dropped and I smiled. What I was dreaming, I realized, was coming true. I can't forget one of the dreams I had, it was a person that was in front of me but while I looked at the clothes the person wore, I could see that it was light clothing, like gray pants and I could see a big van pulling up and it was blue, but the van was one of those that had light around it and TV inside. Months went by and I kept thinking about the dream; it was so real.

More months went by. Then in the summer of 2001 my brother Ferdie rented a mobile home to go on a vacation. Ferdie and his wife and my mother and my niece and nephew's and I were all going to Virginia for the first time. While Ferdie was driving we were passing through New York City. We got stuck in traffic and I thought it would be cool to see a relative of ours. While Ferdie kept driving, after we got away from all the traffic not far from New York, he decided to stop in a rest area. My sister in law Marie and I went inside the little store when a man came over to me and hugged me. I did not know who he was and I kept looking at him and looking at him. I looked toward Marie and said I don't know this man that hugged me.

It turns out I did know him; he was my cousin Maria T. Vazquez's oldest son Freddy. I didn't recognize him because the last time I saw him he was a little boy. It was amazing, one minute you are thinking it would be cool to see a family member from New York City and the next you really do see a relative. My sister in law Marie looked at me and said, "You lucky you have never changed your look the same for him to recognize you in a heartbeat."

I laughed and we took him to see my mother who had stayed in the motor home with the kids. I didn't say anything. At the moment my mother saw her nephew Freddy she jumped up and hugged him. I guess I was the only one that did not remember who Freddy was. Then on that same day while Ferdie started to drive again after a while it was getting late so I decided to go to bed. I was sleeping when I overheard Ferdie telling our mother that he was getting tired. He parked and while everyone went to bed, I remember my mother was fixing her bed when I got up and asked her for a cup of water. I drank it and gave her the cup back and went back to sleep.

My mother settled in for the night. I dozed off after drinking the cup of water but then I started to hear people arguing while I was asleep. I thought the argument was right outside the motor home. I remember I shouted, "Shut up!" but at that exact moment I heard a man trying to talk to me, I got scared that I didn't hear what he was trying to tell me. I started to pray. "Please, Jesus, help me." Then I heard the lady that was arguing start to talk to me, but this time I let her talk to me. The lady told me her description of herself I do remember she told me, I am Theresa and I come from the best school" and she said she came from Paris. I opened my eyes and I saw a portal closing, when I saw that I screamed at my mother telling her **"THEY TALK TO ME!" "THEY TALK TO ME!"**

My mother looked at me and asked, "How?" If I just finished giving you the cup of water. It has not been two seconds since you closed your eyes." The next morning my brother Ferdie found me sleeping with the kids. I never forgot that night.

The rest of vacation was fun and when it was time to go back home, I still wondered why the lady talked to me and I wondered who she was and I wonder who was the guy. What did he try to tell me? I guess I will never know. In 2002 once again I found myself in my bedroom on the computer. It was around four o'clock in the afternoon when I heard the emergence bell ringing. It was coming from the bathroom. As I heard the bell, I did jump but I did not get up from my chair. I didn't know why but I shouted out, "Shut off the bell, don't play with that!" Not a second later it was turned off. I knew it had to be the angel because I was alone in my apartment. I soon realized I was spending too much money on the light bulbs. I got so tired of the light bulb burning out. I kept putting a new light bulb in the lamp. Like I said, it was in the bathroom, living room, hallway and in the kitchen.

One day while watching TV I saw a channel about a psychic and that moment the psychic said you can ask them to stop playing with anything that the spirit is doing at that moment. One day as I went into the bathroom the light went out and I remember at that moment what the psychic said so I shouted please stop. I don't have a lot of money to keep buying light bulbs. To my surprise they did stop. As I sit here writing it's been a few months that the light bulb has not blown out. So far, my apartment has been quiet, the spirit and no light bulb blown out. And the boy has not jumped on my bed for a few weeks. Still I'm searching for answers why this was happening to me and why I was seeing shadows? To my surprise, I found out who in my family had this spiritual gift like I call it. I found out in a way I was not expecting days went by. Again no one knew but once again tragedy was heading our way.

Grandmother

In 2002, my mother called her mother Blanca like clock-work to see how she was doing. My mother Nellie soon realized that she didn't like the way my grandmother sounded. And as soon as Nellie hang up the phone, she called all her sister's Carmelina, Rolanda and Darcie and brothers to tell them she did not like how my grandmother sounded. As everyone got concerned my Aunt Darcie decided to go to Puerto Rico to check up on my grandmother, and grandfather Luis. Before my Aunt Darcie got to Puerto Rico, my grandmother went to the doctor and got x-rays to see what was wrong.

For some reason the doctors or whoever was giving her the test results were taking too long, two weeks had gone by with no test results. By the time, my Aunt Darcie got to Puerto Rico my grandmother was very weak and so sick with no one knowing how sick she was. When my Aunt Darcie brought her parents back to Boston, I picked them up from the airport. When I saw my grandmother for a second, I saw her entire body yellow but I looked away and when I looked back, I saw her regular tan color again. While I kept looking at her, I said to myself; Mom is not going to be happy when she sees her. I drove them to my Aunt Rolanda's house in Boston. My grandmother looked so pale, and so skinny when we got to my aunt's house, and we took my grandparents to the bedroom to rest. When my Aunt Carmelina and my mother walked into my aunt's house, I looked at my mother and my aunt and said, "Be strong, don't look sad in front of Grandmother."

When my mother walked into the bedroom the first words that my grandmother said to her daughter was, "I came to stay." When Blanca told her daughter, I came to stay those words were chilling because what happened next no one had ever expected. The family took my grandmother to the hospital in Brookline, Mass to check on her health. We all found out what was happening to her. She had cancer in the small intestines; the doctor told the family that to save her life she needed chemotherapy. No one wanted for my grandmother to suffer so the family decided not to tell her why she was getting chemotherapy; the family told her she needed chemo to get better from a strange illness she had.

My grandmother stayed in the hospital for four months. Blanca did get better, but it was a long process and every single member of the family, aunt, uncles, took turns staying overnight in the hospital with my grandmother. Blanca was getting better, when I went to visit her. During the visit, I asked my grandmother if she knew of anyone in the family who could see spirits or as I called it "a gift." To my surprise my grandmother looked at me and said, "Yes, I know who," as I looked at her so surprised that she knew who had the gift. My grandmother told me her mother Conchita and her grandmother Eliza. At that moment in time I finally found some answers. Even though I was very sad over what was happening to my grandmother I was glad that I finally got some answers. For me to know why I was experiencing this at least it lifted pressure of my chest. Now I know that I have a spiritual gift of some kind by seeing or feeling things when the spirit is around me, but no one expected what was going to happen next. Time went on; it was hard for all of the grandkids that knew what was happening.

We all took time to see "Mamamita" as all grandkids called our grandmother. We were sad because all of the grandkids did not grow up close to my grandmother Mamamita. She lived in Puerto Rico, and we got to see her when we took a trip to Puerto Rico or Mamamita came here to see us. While my grandmother Blanca kept getting chemotherapy, and a few months went by, when we all heard that the chemotherapy did work, the cancer did go away. In May 2002 Blanca was well to come out of the hospital and stayed with her daughter Carmelina in Brookline, Massachusetts.

Blanca started to get so well that hair that she lost by the chemotherapy started to come back. Then in June 2002 Blanca was strong enough to visit family members. Our surprise came in June 2002, my grandmother Blanca traveled to stay with my mother's house in New Hampshire. Blanca began to eat again and she enjoyed playing with her great-grandkids. One of the great-grandkids that she laughed a lot with was Brant, who was two years old at the time. Blanca also played with her other great-grandkids Kyle and Dede and her grandson Gino. Meanwhile, my grandfather Luis was happy his wife was well again and next to him. On June 20, 2002 I went to my mother's house to have a talk with my grandmother "Mamamita."

While we sat in the kitchen talking, I was looking at her and at that moment my ears started to ring, and I started to see the glitter behind her. I looked at her and I could see more glitter forming around her; I told her what I saw behind her. My grandmother asked if I could see who it was and I said I believed is an angel. I wish I could see better to tell who it was; I did try my best but as fast as the glitter came it went way.

Days went by and my grandmother Blanca loved life, she was trying to get her strength back in her legs and she tried to walk around the neighborhood. Then on July 4, 2002 my grandmother was enjoying a beautiful summer day while having fun and laughing at her great-grandson Brant's playfulness. And the day began great the family was getting ready to watch the fireworks and we were outside of my mother's house. For some reason, my grandmother went back inside the house, and a few minutes had passed when my mother heard her mother screaming and calling out for her daughter Nellie, shouting that, she had fallen down.

We all heard my mother say, "Is that my mom shouting?" as, I ran in, and my friend Hollis ran in after me my brother Ferdie passed me and picked my grandmother up from the floor. She had tripped over her slippers because she didn't have feeling in her legs from the chemo and didn't have too much strength. When my brother Ferdie put our grandmother on the bed she began to complain that she'd hit her side of her stomach; I asked where she hit herself, and my grandmother pointed it out. It was her left side of the stomach. So, days went by, and my mother kept checking her mother making sure that my grandmother kept eating.

My mother soon noticed her mother was not eating. While Blanca was not eating as much food as she was supposed to, my mother got worried and called her sister Carmelina and told her that their mother was not eating again. My Aunt Carmelina came to get her for a doctor checkup. The news spread fast: my grandmother's cancer came back again in her small intestines and this time my grandmother was told by her kids what she had.

The doctor told the family they could not help anymore and that if they gave her chemotherapy it wouldn't do any good; the cancer had spread. The doctor told the family they could not help anymore, just take her home and wait for her to die. Those words were the hardest words for anyone. It's unbelievable to see a loved one go through the pain, and the only thing you can do is watch from the side line waiting for her suffering to begin. You can't do anything about it to stop it and just pray that she won't suffer a lot. Everyone did not live so close to one another. Some of the family member homes were in Brockton, Mass, New York City, New Hampshire, and Puerto Rico.

Like my grandmother's sister Delia who came to see her from Puerto Rico to spend time with her. Even her niece Lillian from New York came to see her. We were all talking, when Lillian happened to say she had a tattoo of an angel on her back shoulder. When I saw it, I don't know why but I said to her, "Oh cool, the angels are watching over you." Lillian looked at me and said, "Yeah, I know because I see them." That blew my mind, I didn't know she had the gift too. I asked her for telephone number, that I needed to talk to her and get some information. Every one of Blanca's grandchildren came to see, from the oldest to the youngest and great-grandchildren. Then one day while I was home, I went to bed, and I started to dream but the dream became peaceful and kind of strange. I started to see a light in front of me and then it started to open up wide as I kept seeing the light opening up. Then I saw a lot of people waiting in front of the light, they looked like they were waiting for someone to come through the light; it looked like the light of heaven and it was an amazing site to see. And the dream was so very peaceful.

I kept thinking about it, and I realized it was my grandmother's family waiting for her on the other side, an amazing dream it was for me. Meanwhile, the family took their time to make all Blanca's wishes come true. Whatever my grandmother wanted; they all gave it to her. We saw my grandmother little by little slipping away. She always did something every day at 3:00 p.m. she prayed the rosary. On August 12, 2002 her daughter's Carmelina told her sister Nellie and her grand aunt Delia, let's pray the rosary. They started to pray the rosary next to their mother Blanca, meanwhile, my three younger cousins Gino, Darin and Xadrien were in the living room. August 12, 2002 is a day we will never forget. While praying the rosary, what happened next, I won't ever forget. While my mother and my aunts were praying, I was driving on the highway in New Hampshire.

I saw a shadow pass behind me, I saw it in the rear-view mirror. I didn't understand until my cell phone rang. It was a friend telling me that my mother called crying, looking for me. When I called her, she was crying that my grandmother just passed away. That's when I understood why I saw a shadow. It happened while they were praying the rosary; they started the rosary at 3:00 p.m. and at 3:30 p.m. Blanca took her last breath. A few seconds before the phone rang, I saw the shadow; I believe my grandmother came into my car to say goodbye to me. Blanca did love to be with her children and she spent her last days with her entire family. Even her grandchildren, at least she did get a chance to know her grandchildren and her great-grandchildren. Even though some of the great-grandkids were too young to remember who Blanca was. For the small generation, we will keep her memory alive for everyone to know who Blanca Andujar "Mamamita" was.

On August 15, 2002 the family took my grandmother Blanca to her home town of Florida, Puerto Rico. And on August 16, 2002 at 3:30 p.m., Blanca Andujar was laid to rest. I had never been to a funeral in Puerto Rico I had heard about the funeral but to see it in person was different and amazing for me. The family members march behind the hearse and we were coming out of the funeral home. I saw a car with big speakers on top playing a song that she loved so much when the hearse drove and we started to march. When we got to the cemetery and we all sat to give our last respects, some people got up to talked about my grandmother. I saw a man get up and play the accordion. That was her favorite instrument. She wanted to learn how to play it but never learned.

MAMAMITA LAST MOTHER DAY WITH US 2000

Blanca Andujar was loved by everyone

The last picture Blanca took with her son Edward this picture was taking 2 days before her death.
BLANCA ANDUJAR AGE 77
September 17, 1921- August 15, 2001

My trip to Sabana Grande

Months went by, and the family began to heal from the sadness, but for me I kept going back to the same thing. I kept feeling my hair being touched, and the boy kept jumping on my bed. But the phone stopped ringing for a while. Then my mother and her sister Carmelina and Carmelina's grand-daughter, Casie and I decided to go to Puerto Rico, for the first anniversary of my grandmother's death. It was hard for all of us; we were going to stay at my grandmother's house.

She was the one who was always waiting at the door for us to arrive, but it was hardest for my mother. She was so over-whelmed with grief because she didn't go to Puerto Rico, for her mother's funeral she couldn't face it. And for the first anniversary it was much harder getting out of the car and finding an empty house even though my grandfather Luis was there. But to see he was alone was harder for my mother to bear. We stayed for three weeks in Puerto Rico, and I also got a chance to see my brothers and sister.

When I arrived in Puerto Rico, as usual, I called my sister to tell her I was in town. I got the surprise of my life! My sister Diana was pregnant. I was so happy with the news that I was going to be an aunt for the 11th time. I am happy being an aunt. Then I got an invitation from my grandfather Luis' next-door neighbors. Rosa and her family invited me to take a trip to a place in Puerto Rico called Sabana Grande. In English it is called "Big blanket." The story goes that the Virgin Mary appeared to a man there. As soon as I heard that story, I said yes, I would like to go.

The next day we went, and it was a two-hour ride to Sabana Grande. My sister Diana also went with me. During the ride Diana and I talked almost the whole time as we had to, we catch up with everything we have done. When we got there and walked in, it was an amazing feeling. As you keep walking there was a building it had a lot of walkers, braces, crutches, and special shoes. It was all behind a glass wall showing how many people were cured. Thousands of Miracles had happened there. We walked inside the place for a while; we looked around. I went to get some holy water only to find a long line.

We were in the line. I was next to my sister Diana and my cousin, Casie and a family friend's granddaughter, Karla. While waiting and looking around I happened to smell roses. I turned to my sister Diana and asked her if she smelled the roses; then I turned to Casie to ask her if she smelled the roses. As soon as, I asked Karla, the family friend, when everyone said yes, they smelled the roses, the smell vanished, and we could not smell it anymore. The only thing about it was; that there were no roses anywhere. After I drank the holy water and poured holy water over my head and put some next to my right ear, I could not hear from that ear very well. Then I ran to tell my mother what had happened to us.

We all smelled roses, and it vanished as soon as everyone said yes. Then I said I believe it was the Virgin Mary wanted us to know she was around us. After a while in the park we were ready to go when I found out that the guy that the Virgin Mary appeared to was going to talk about his experience. I found out it was the 50th anniversary to the day that the Virgin Mary appeared to him.

A few of us sat down to see if he came to talk but we had to go. The driver who took us to Sabana Grande was worried that it would rain because his wipers in the van were not working, so we left not hearing the man's story. We drove back but to everyone's surprise, it never rained. I was talking about how strange it was that there were no roses anywhere, and we all smelled the roses.

This is the entrance of the Sabana Grande.
In English it is called "Big blanket."

When we got back to my Grandfather Luis' house, my great Aunt Delia asked us to go to her house for dinner. My great Aunt Delia was trying her best to make sure her niece's Nellie and Carmelina not feel alone without their mother Blanca.

While we had one more day to go, and we had everyone over at my grandfather's house, my Aunt Delia was walking up the stairs. When I got up to go in the house for something when I looked toward my Aunt Delia at that moment that she was walking up the stairs, I had to take a double look because the first time it looked like it was someone else. It was like I was seeing another lady walking up the stairs. My Aunt Delia was by herself at that moment. I took a second look, and it was her again. Everyone was together that day at my Grandfather Luis' house, we had fun laughing at everyone's, jokes. Then later that night we got ready to go back to New Hampshire. The next day we got a phone call that my grand Aunt Delia went to the bathroom in the middle of the night and found herself bleeding heavily. Her daughter Ivette took her to the hospital.

We got our suitcases ready, but we went to the hospital to see her. She was happy and smiling. We saw that she looked okay and that she had to stay overnight. But we had to catch a flight. While back home we kept checking up on Delia to see how she was doing. She is the last generation of my grandmother's sisters and brother. When I got back home, I began to think back at what we did in Puerto Rico, and I realized something. I talked to my mother about me knowing I was smelling roses that day when we went to Sabana Grande. I also remember going to my brother Cesar's house. As I sat there talking to my sister in law Yamir Mendez, I told her about what was happening in my house. I was seeing spirits go by so fast that when she told me some of her stories, to my surprise my brother Cesar had the gift. Even his wife did but I did not know how their gift worked because everyone has different spiritual gifts even though they don't practice their gift by reading anyone. I also spent time with my wonderful niece and nephew while I was there.

I guess my vacation was over as soon, as I walked into my bedroom, I could see that the spirit was welcoming me home. I laughed because as soon as I went into my bedroom, a flash of light streaked across the room like they were saying, "I am still here." And I still slept with the light on. I soon understood, I was back from my vacation. The boy started to jump on my bed like he was trying to say, "I am still here too."

One of my first dream predictions

Then in October of 2002 I went to sleep and I started to dream about my grand Aunt Delia. She was standing in front of her house on her porch. But at the same time I heard a voice telling me she will be dead in one year. I did not get scared of the dream but I did think about it. I did end up telling my friend Mayra about the dream. I told her what I saw in a dream, and heard the voice telling me she will be die in a year. I remember Mayra telling me sometimes the dreams are telling you someone who is far from you will die. I looked at Mayra and said, "But that is the problem.

My Aunt Delia lives in Puerto Rico, now that is far away." I did not tell anyone else about the dream especially since my mother is a nervous person. To my surprise one year later, the last of my grandmother's generation, one year later after having my dream, Delia Hernandez died. She died October 28, 2002 at the age of 81 one years after her sister Blanca's death. My Aunt Delia death was strange because no one knew what kind of sickness she had for her to die. Top it all off one of the doctors gave her the wrong dose of medicine. After that Delia began to go downhill. So when they tried to fix the problem Delia never recovered. She died in her daughter Laura's house close to the rest of her children's Nilda, Onil and Ivette.

This picture is exactly like the dream
I had my Aunt Delia on her porch

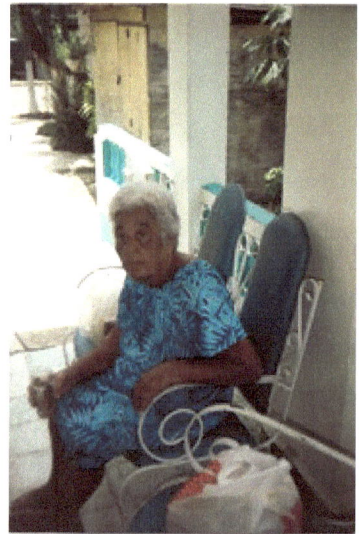

Delia Hernandez

October 28, 2002 at the age of 81

Seeing and feeling things around me

Since the little boy showed himself to me I still feel him jumping on my bed and I still feel my hair being touched. I got used to it. Each day is different but I have learned not to run out of my apartment. The light bulb doesn't blow out as much anymore. People still come over to see the door and it's been six years since it all started, while I went on with my life one day at it time. One night I was sleeping when I woke up to a feeling of someone putting a covering over me but it was not my blanket.

I felt a warm feeling I opened my eyes. I felt it, I knew it was a cover from the spirit world. I smiled and kept sleeping. Then on Christmas Day 2005 my brother Ferdie and his wife Marie gave me a present for Christmas. It was a brass clock that had angels on the side. I loved it because I collected angels, when I put it on top of the entertainment center. Soon after I put the battery in the clock. I sat down to watch TV when I heard a bell ringing on the clock. I said, "oh it has a bell in it and it rings each hour" not thinking any different. I got up and looked at the clock, and to my surprise. There was "NO ALARM!" The clock wasn't supposed to ring at all. I got a spooky feeling that came over me but I kept the clock for a while.

Every time I watched TV, however, I felt unease. I felt uncomfortable around the clock. I told my mother that the clock rang every hour and I could not find the alarm. I kept the clock because it was a gift from my brother and his wife. Then in 2005, I took a vacation that I really needed. I got invited by my father, Carmelo to visit him.

He now was living in Saint Croix, Virgin Islands. I had not seen my father for a long time. When he asked me to go to visit him I jumped and said yes. I'd never been to Saint Croix. I went and stayed with my youngest brother Angel and his wife Elizabeth. I was happy because I got the chance to know my sister in law Elizabeth. I was grateful knowing who she was and I also was glad to get to know my nephew Pablito and my niece Vivian. I have to say I never in my life had been snorkeling under-water. I found it so peaceful and nice to watch the fish. To see what is under the ocean is a different world, and I loved it. I would do it again in a heartbeat.

My father Carmelo worked the whole time I was with him. He even decided to send for the rest of his grandkids from Puerto Rico to spend time with me not having seen them growing up. I had a chance to see them and spent three weeks with them. I spent time with my three nephews Pablito, Jorge, Kyle and my two nieces Vivian and Gemini. Then after one week with the kids and my sister in law Elizabeth, my father sent for my sister Diana with her baby daughter Estrella. It was a blast seeing all of them and getting to know each one of them. The day came when my vacation in Saint Croix came to an end. I took a small airplane to get to a bigger plane in Puerto Rico but when I landed in Puerto Rico the other plane was delayed more than four hours.

It was taking off again at 6:30 p.m. I called Carmelo and told him I will not be calling him from Boston. I have to be in Puerto Rico for a few hours so he decided to call my sister Diana. That had left a few days before I did.

Diana picked me up with her daughter Estrella and her mother Alejandra and I spent time with them. Those were a short few hour but I had fun talking to my sister's mother Alejandra. When I got back to New Hampshire, the Fourth of July was over and I never got to see the fire works for the first time in my life. After putting everything away in my bedroom I laughed because I had not been in my apartment for more than a few minutes and the sparkles started. I guess they wanted me to know I was home and they wanted me to know they were still around. A few weeks went by when my brother Cesar called me. He wanted to move to New Hampshire.

My brother Cesar and his wife Yamir got their apartment and they also helped me understand a little more about this gift as I call it. I know how it works as I got to know more and understand it. Watching my sister in law Marie, now I had another sister in law, Yamir. I understood that when the spirits want you to know they are there and want to talk to you, they do anything to make sure you feel their presence. After a while I changed the living room and put the clock that my brother Ferdie gave me on the table before Cesar and his wife moved in. They stayed with me for a few months. But I soon realized my brother Cesar also felt strange around the clock too. When Yamir told me, I looked at her very happy. I told her, "**THANK GOD!**"

I was not the only one who felt strange around the clock. That's when I took the clock and gave it away. My sister in law Yamir felt and also saw the little boy and let his presence be known to them even trying to play with the kids Sergio and Vivi.

A month went by and my sister in law Yamir also felt a lot of presence in the building and I knew that because my sister in law Marie felt a man's presence in the elevator every time she came over. I only saw sparkles when I was in the elevator or the main lobby of the building. I can only see a lot of sparkles. I guess I was used seeing the sparkles but wanted to know why I keep seeing them and what it meant. So, I began to read all type of Psychic and Medium books. As I began to read this story written by John Holland his story looked similar to what I had experienced. He too had also seen sparkles. So, I continued reading all types of books. Then one day my brother and his wife were still staying with me. They went out for the day and I was home alone.

When I was sitting in the living room watching TV a white feather came down in front of me. I was amazed about seeing the feather and how it come down in front of me. I remember telling my sister Yamir but she smiled and said oh wow but I didn't make a big deal out of it even though I knew and everyone knew I don't have a bird and did not have anything in my apartment that had feather. I smiled because I realized that I know now the angels are with me. One day I had dream and from the first I thought it was just a dream. Because it felt real, however, I never forgot it. The dream was about a person who was in front of me and I saw that the person was wearing light clothes. A blue van pulled up in front me.

I can describe the van. It had a television inside. At the time I started to see that the dream I was having sometimes came out true and it's like they are so real that you never can get them out of your mind. I actually told someone about the dream though I can't recall who. I mentioned the dream too but I knew it was a lady.

I remember her responding by saying I know what you mean. and dreams are just that, dreams. I responded by saying the problem is that most of my dreams are coming true. Then one day in 2006 I had a dream and, in the dream, I saw my brother Cesar and his wife Yamir moving away. The way the dream played out I figured out that the dream is like someone moving out of town. I saw them getting a house and I heard a voice tell me four. I could not hear all of it completely well but I did tell Yamir. I told her it was someone else in my dream. I did not want to tell her she was in my dream, I wanted to see if it came true. Then One day in 2007 my brother Cesar called me and asked if I wanted to go out and take a ride with him and his wife and the kids. I was home doing nothing so I said sure why not. I went down to the lobby to wait for them to show up. When I saw what they had pulled up in I was shocked! My dream had come true. I laughed but at that moment I didn't tell them anything. To my surprise it was the exact van I saw in my dream and my brother had the same exact clothes on that I saw in the dream. Well what else will I be dreaming about that will come true?

The year I will never forget

To my surprise in May 2007, I got a spiritual reading by my sister in law Yamir. She told me I would hear the spirits soon. I looked at her and said, "Really?" Then she said a few other things like I'm going to be reading people, like she was reading me. As I sat back she said, "I will hear my spirit guide." Then a few days later I talked to my cousin, Mildred Ortiz who I got to know by phone calls I also found out Mildred had her own spiritual calling. While we were talking, Mildred told me that 2007 will be my year. A month went by, and I never forgot what Mildred told me about 2007 being my year. One day I was home meditating. About 20 minutes into my meditation I overheard a lady's voice telling me "YOU CAN DO IT." I heard that, and I jumped up out of my meditation. I was not expecting to hear the voice. I even told my mother what the voice said. "I could do it."

My mother said, "oh that is spooky." My mother told me she doesn't know how I could live alone with what I went through, seeing the boy and the shadows. I quickly told her I think if I move out I will still have this spiritual gift. Where ever I go, if I'm living at my apartment or I am living with a person I believe won't be any different. I think it is a spiritual journey. I even told my sister in law Yamir what the voice had said to me, "You can do it." Yamir asked me, "Do what?" I said, how should I know? "All I know is what the voice said." Then one day I was asleep but I kept shaking my head three or four times because whoever was trying to talk to me should have spoken louder because I was sleepy.

Then in January 2007 my brother Cesar told me he bought a house in a different state. I looked at him and remembered my dream again came to reality. They were moving across the country. I had learned somewhere to get myself a Pendulum because it was easy to get answers just by letting it move on its own so I did. On July 5, 2007 I was at my kitchen table asking yes and no question with a Pendulum. And in asking any of the questions would the Pendulum move. Yes, it did move to a few questions. And yes, sometimes it didn't move at all.

While I was new using the Pendulum, I wanted to ask a question again just writing down my question. If the Pendulum moved one way it would mean yes or if it moved a different way, it meant no. Everything changed on July 10, 2007. I heard a couple of words and as I kept writing the spirit kept spelling letters out. As the day went on I kept writing letters and I didn't know what they wanted to say. I remember the next day. On July 11, 2007 I got a call from my sister in law Yamir, and I mentioned to her I heard my spiritual guide talk to me.

Yamir requested to write whatever they tell me. As I said to her, "I have the time, I'm living alone. I can hear them clear," so I did what Yamir recommended and wrote what they told me. By now I was hearing them much clearer. But I kept it to myself. I kept it from my mother and even from my family members. I did not know why but I needed to see first what they wanted to tell me, I didn't even tell any of my friends. I know my family would not understand at this moment in time. I did thank Yamir for the help she gave me, spiritual guidance. Yamir knew more than I ever did and for her to help me was nice. I knew she gave me spiritual advice and she didn't use her special ability at any time.

I was beginning to realize and understand that this gift is hard. Besides it doesn't come with directions. I tried my best to learn from reading Angel's, Psychic and Medium books. I even tried reading the Bible even though I was a person that who was still learning how to pray the rosary. I never knew that what was about to start would change my life forever and change me spiritually, mentally, and physically. I grew up more than I ever imagined.

When the light changed me

I kept writing each letter but still didn't know what they were trying to say. Until I could get one whole word, until I could hear each sentence clear. I realized while I was in my bedroom, my ear kept ringing. It was different, like I never felt before. It was incredible! I guess that's how I knew when they wanted me to write. I was okay with it. I was not scared at all, but I saw the boy once more time, this time next to my bedroom door. But not as clear as the first time I saw him and no I never asked him what he wanted. But I did realize what I was writing was predictions, and while writing everything down they were telling me I never thought of asking them any questions.

On July 26, 2007 I got so scared when I could not understand why I did not hear a voice, but I started hearing a lot of voices. I heard perhaps a dozen voices or more. Screaming, shouting, telling me, **"HE IS COMING! HE IS COMING!"** over and over. I knew it was totally different when I started to cry, I could not tell my mother. She didn't even know that I could hear my spiritual guide talking to me in the first place. For some reason, I thought if I tell my sister in law Yamir she won't understand what happened to me. That is exactly what ran through my mind. I didn't even think of asking my brother Cesar, or my sister in law Marie for that matter. I kept thinking no one will understand. I thought no one can't help me with that answer. I felt I had to go and find somewhere else the answer. I was at home crying my eyes out. I was so scared out of my mind.

I started to think the worst thing ever, that I could have mental illness, schizophrenia. While I thought about having a mental illness I started to hearing, from my spirit guide. **"YOU DON'T HAVE THAT. YOU DON'T HAVE MENTAL ILLNESS. YOU ARE A NORMAL PERSON."** The more the voices talked to me the more I cried, while the voices kept saying, **"HE IS COMING. HE IS COMING."** I stopped writing the prediction down after I heard the dozens of voices. I felt so alone at this point. I could not tell my family. I believed they would have also thought the worst possible thing. I had lost it. So, I never said a word and that's when I started to go to all the Catholic churched until I got in one church that the city closed down in New Hampshire. Somehow, I got in, and the only thing I found was the statue of the Virgin Mary. I sat down in front of her and started to **"SHOUT"** at her in Spanish. "Mother of mine please **"HELP ME!"** I am so scared.

What is happening to me? Please, you are our mother Virgin Mary, please help me!" I even called out for her son Jesus Christ: "Please help me! I am so scared." After an hour of being inside the church, I went back home. The more I cried. Then I decided to go to the only place I could think of. I decided to go to Pepperel, Massachusetts. ("I am back to the beginning when I started telling my mother's my story.") On January 28, 2008 at twelve in the afternoon I went to my mother's house, and she started to explain to me the way I was acting. That August of 2007 I was acting strangely and my eyes were so wide open it was like I saw a ghost or something. That's when she started to get so worried about me because I looked lost.

So, I started to explain why I never told her what really happened to me on August 1, 2007. We both were sitting in my mother's bedroom when I began telling her what happened and what I saw. And why I was acting "strangely." This is where everything started. On July 5, 2007 I began to hear my spirit guide talk to me and I started to write down everything the spirit guides was telling me. I began realizing what I was writing was so many predictions. One of the predictions was that the Red Sox will win the World Series and in 2007 to my surprise it came true. I kept talking to my mother that I kept writing and writing so many predictions until the end of July 26, 2007. I was fine.

I heard my spiritual guide speaking to me and I was not scared; besides, I was hearing only one voice. But after that everything changed. I started to hear not one voice, but I started to hear a lot of voices shouting, "**HE IS COMING! HE IS COMING!**" over and again. I didn't know what to think, so I got so scared. I thought oh my God why am I hearing something different. I got so scared I didn't know who to turn to, and I started going to church again, church after church. I guess I felt I was searching for something. I believe looking for some protection. I was so scared I began to cry, and I became panicked and ran to different churches. I never thought of asking my spiritual guide why I was hearing so many voices. I was so scared that I cried more; I ran back and forth from my house, to the church.

Then on August 1, 2007 I decided to go to Pepperel, Massachusetts, where there is an altar of the statue of Fatima and a big, picture of Jesus Christ. When I got there, I was crying.

I stood crying in front of the picture of Jesus Christ begging Him to help me. I was so scared. What was happening to me? At one point I screamed out, "What kind of gift is this? If this is what is supposed to happen?" I could not stop crying and kept asking Jesus to help me. I was so scared out of my mind. After I finished praying and I happened to look next to the big picture of Jesus, where another picture of Jesus hung, except that the second picture was of only His face. I walked over to the picture, and for some reason, I touched it. I then looked at my left hand and touched my right hand, with which I had touched the picture. Not knowing why, I did that. I soon realized I had been there for a couple of hours. I remembered I left around six or seven in the evening. I remember I was calmed and began to drive.

I realized I did not hear much of the voices as I drove back home to New Hampshire Route 111 for some reason. I looked out my driver side window and when I was looking, I saw the sun, but it was looking completely different. I kept looking. I saw the sun changing; it had rays shooting out so many colors coming straight down, red, yellow, green, and others colors all around the sun. Then the sun started jumping around like it was dancing, then suddenly it looked like a dark moon went over it like an eclipse. That's when I stopped the car to see better. What I saw was amazing and out of this world. It was beautiful and surprising to me but what "**SHOCKED**" me was, someone was coming toward me with His hands wide open. I saw "**JESUS CHRIST**," that's who I saw coming towards me! With His hands wide open I could see His face, His white robe, I saw His brown hair His brown beard.

He came down toward me, then He vanished. I was shocked at what I had just witnessed. It was shocking and amazing. What happened at that very moment? I parked by the side of the road for a few more minutes. I could not believe what I just saw. I didn't tell anyone what I witnessed. I was too shocked. I just saw Jesus Christ. I went home and began to cry, but I felt different. I started feeling a lot differently. I started to write again but not a lot; one day I even heard my Aunt Gladys, she passed away 1997. But I can't remember what she told me. I wrote more prediction but I kept crying. Then on August 18, 2007 I heard a voice through my crying, I heard "GO TO CHURCH." I got up and went to the first church I saw. In the church I sat in the front row seat. While sitting and waiting for the mass to start I began to see sparkles. That's when it was clear to me what I was witnessing. The Virgin of Guadalupe, show herself to me and at the same time I could see clear as day the Sacred Heart and a lot of little angels at that very moment.

After I left the church I went straight to my mother's house. I could not take it anymore. I told her what I saw at the church that Virgin Guadalupe, the Sacred Heart and a lot of little Angels appeared to me. I began to cry, telling her, everything and at that very moment I could hear my spiritual guide. I was trying to explain to my mother when my niece Dede walk into the dining room. I didn't want to talk in front of her but my mother kept telling me explain. She said, "Ok Dede can stay." I began to tell my mother at that moment that I saw Jesus, and I started to hear my spiritual guide but my mother did not understand. She did not want to look at me.

When I heard the guide tell me what my niece Dede was thinking, I repeated everything. The guide kept telling me what Dede was thinking and every time I got it right. Every time I got it right Dede kept asking me, "How do you know what I am thinking?" I just wanted to see if I was right, but I did not know what I was doing because a day later my mother told me that my niece Dede was scared of me. I knew at the time I did wrong by telling Dede what she was thinking. I just wanted my mother to know I was hearing my angels and I guess this gift don't come with instructions. After that happened, I started feeling so different again. Though I felt different after seeing Jesus coming to me, I started see double. Like I was in my body, but I was seeing through someone else's eyes. I walked down Main Street touching the walls. I touched every building I came upon; I felt like I had to walk everywhere.

I knew the building was old, but I felt I needed to walk. I kept seeing through someone else's eyes. For some reason I felt the need to touch the building because I felt they were brand new not knowing why I felt that way. Then; I started to write in Spanish. I started to write poems, then I started to have so much strength that I started to clean my apartment. When I got up in the morning at that exact moment, I started to clean and go to bed late every day. I threw out everything that was in my house.

I felt the need that I had to throw out everything old. I even went to my mother's house at one point and went to the attic where I had a trunk full of old stuff that I collected and threw all of it out. I also started to let the water in the kitchen sink run all day long. Also, in the bathroom and even the tub and the bathroom sink for three or four days straight not knowing why I had to do it.

Then I decided to throw out the bookcase that was behind the door to my bedroom. Then a day past I was moping around the apartment, and when I went to mope behind the door in my bedroom, I saw a hand on the wall but the problem was I never touch the wall. When I looked again, I was seeing a hand and in the middle of the palm I saw the Virgin Mary. I don't know why, but I went out in the hallway to see if anyone was out there. I saw Paula, and I told her she needed to see something. Then I went straight to Bertha's apartment and knocked on her door. I told Bertha to follow me to my apartment.

When they both came to my apartment, I ushered them into my bedroom. When I showed Bertha and Paula the wall, I asked what they saw. Bertha looked at Paula and said, "I see the hand but what is incredible is, it's got the Virgin Mary inside the hand." Then Bertha took two steps forward and put her hand close to the wall. The hand was the same size as Bertha's. When she stepped back, Bertha looked at me and said, "It came with me." I looked and the print of the hand on the wall had vanished, and I responded by telling Bertha it was for you. I remember mopping the floor. I remember they left my apartment after that as I keep cleaning and cleaning nonstop.

One day I got undressed to take a shower, but I know for some reason I put on a white vest I had in the closet. I can't explain why, I had to put it on. I went in the tub, but I keep seeing flashes in my head when Jesus Christ was getting baptized in the river. When I got out of the tube, I wondered how could I "mock" Jesus Christ. I began to cry how I could I do such a thing.

To a respectable man how could I mock my religion that I grew up in. I cried so much that day. I restarted to clean my house. Once again, I left my apartment, and I was driving up Main Street and my car ran out of gas. I parked on Canal Street next to the parking lot of Dunkin Donuts. I walked all the way to my mother's house. I remember my mother Nellie, her sister Rolanda and even her sister in law Maria were in the living room.

When I sat down for a few minutes, I felt like for me, it was too many people talking, at the same time. When I sat down for a few minutes, I felt like for me, it was too many people talking, at the same time. But the facts are it was only three people in the living room. I began to tell my Aunt Rolanda a joke. I thought I said it right, but my mother told the rest of the joke, but the way she said it I thought I was not right. I thought, ok maybe my brother Ferdie said it to my mother a different way. I know I looked at my Aunt Rolanda and I shrugged. It was changed. I think ten minutes passed before I told my mother that my car was in the Dunkin Donuts parking lot because I ran out of gas. We all got in the car and my Aunt Rolanda took me to get some gas at the gas station on Canal Street. At the gas station my aunts and my mother left to go to the store.

I walked from the gas station to my car a block away. When I passed the first building next to Dunkin Donuts, I got to the parking lot and to my surprise I did not see my car in the parking lot. I thought someone had stolen it. I do remember calling my brother Cesar telling him my car got stolen, and I also called my Aunt Rolanda. But I could not get her on the cell phone, so I decided to call her husband Jay. I told him I was trying to reach his wife Rolanda and explain that someone stole my car.

He called his wife to come get me. I felt like I was in the twilight zone. I kept seeing double vision, seeing through someone else's eyes. When I went to get my cell phone again, I could not find it. For some reason I was thinking maybe I left it at the house, but I know I used it a few seconds before so I looked inside my purse and did not find it there. Then a few seconds later I found it in the same pocket that I had looked in a few minutes before. Then I looked and saw I got a phone call by one person about seven times. I knew I did not make them, and as I put the phone back, in my purse I felt I had lost time. Like I was there one minute and the second it was time lapse for me.

As I looked for my cell phone to see if my Aunt Rolanda called me. I tried to find it and again it was not in my purse. I looked and looked. Then I found it inside my pants pocket not knowing how it got there. Then I heard my mother's voice calling me from the other side of the building of the Dunkin Donuts. Pointing and saying, "Come here to the other side of the building to the other side parking lot." My mother said to me, "Your car is right here." I laughed in front of her but inside me I wanted to cry. I felt so lost, like I lost track of time. But I felt His spirit inside me and I said "Him" because I don't dare say that it was "Jesus Christ" that was inside me.

But my mom interrupted me while I was telling her the story and said, "No, Jennie, is the Holy Spirit." I looked at her and said' "OK." But I am the one who felt His presence inside me. I knew I was feeling different and I cannot tell a lie. But then as I kept cleaning my apartment, I threw so many things out that the people in the building saw what I was doing and asked me why I was throwing so much stuff out.

I told them I need to clean. I even started to scream in my apartment "**VICTORY**" "**VICTORY**" all around the house. I could not say why but I had to put my two fingers up screaming "VICTORY!" At one point I realized what I was doing. When I realized what I was doing I looked out the door to see if anyone was coming to knock on my door and ask me what was wrong but no one did. I guess I wanted someone to ask me what was going on with me or something. I guess I was so scared. Then I also remembered close to the end of August, I had collection of statues of all different kinds of angels, I started to give some away. What hurt me was I broke some.

I even broke the statue of Saint Anthony and a few others while I was cleaning. I could not take it anymore, I needed to know why I felt this way. I decided to go to see Jacki Joy the psychic. When I got to the door of her house, I began to cry my eyes out. I asked her to help me. She told me to calm down and explained why I was crying. When I began to explain to her, she told me, "You are hearing a lot of angels, they want you not to worry and not to be scared." I kept hearing the angels, they were using "familiar" voices. Jacki told me to sit down and let them talk to me while she was getting ready to read me. I looked at Jacki and told her, "Jacki, I hear a voice telling me to tell you something."

Jacki got excited and asked, "What they are saying?" I told her. Jacki smiled and told me it was her grandfather that I was giving a message to her. She told me don't worry everything is going to be ok. I left Jacki's house feeling little bit better. I decided to go to my friend Mayra's house to talk to her but she soon realized something was troubling me.

She told me to go to her mother Edelmira Rivera and she would help me out. I know that my car did not have much gas, so I walked to her house. When I got to her house, I looked at Edelmira and began to cry uncontrollably. I told her that I could hear my spirit guide. She also had the gift of seeing, but she stood up and said, "You have in you the fire of the Holy Spirit." Edelmira stood in front of me and started to shake her hand around me for a while. I kept crying. She told me, "Don't worry, everything will be fine." Meanwhile, my mother or my family didn't know yet what was going on with me. I remembered once walking into my mother's house. She asked me where I was going. I told her I was heading later to the bank.

I did not know what day it was for that matter. I didn't remember ever looking at the time at all. Through the entire month of August when she told me it was Saturday in the afternoon. I would look at her so surprised I left. Later I can't recall the hour. Back to my house, but I continued going to church nonstop. Then I remember going to a lady in my building. I knocked on her door and I asked, "Joyce, can I come in I need to speak to you." I sat down and started to cry and told her what was happening to me. As I explained to Joyce Seyer, she even had her special spirituality. While talking, I remember her husband was standing in front of us hearing us talking, but he had his Bible out and was ready to go out to church. I was so out of it at this point, I was scared because I assumed, he was a ghost. As he walked out the door to go to church, I was wondering if she could see him. Why I thought that I don't know. While speaking to Joyce, I remembered I had given her an angel of one of a dozen collection I had.

And I asked for it back and Joyce understood what I was going through and gave it back to me. I guess I was thinking at that moment getting one of my angels back that I could feel protected or not guilty because I broke some of the others. Then as the month of August came to an end, I started to feel myself again but I started to throw holy water on the floor. When I did that, I felt good by what I was doing. So, I kept throwing holy water all over myself and started to pray shouting the name of the Father and the Holy Spirit. Then I poured more holy water all over the house.

Then I went out of my apartment for hours. At the time I was throwing holy water everywhere. I even went to each floor in my building with holy water, I guess I was cleaning the area thinking I was cleaning in spiritual way; I guess I was protecting myself from I don't know what. I keep throwing holy water around the building and by September 2007 I was already myself. But I soon heard my guide talking to me, and at one point she told me, "Jennie, you are not sick you are a normal person." I still was thinking that I dipped myself in the tub; I didn't remember exactly what I had done in the tub, but I kept thinking that I had mocked Jesus Christ.

Then I heard my spiritual guide tell me try to remember you did not dip yourself in the tub. When I heard her telling me that, I began to cry. She said, "You took a shower with a white vest on. You were getting a movie clip in your head of Jesus Crist when He was getting dipped in the river." Even though I kept crying, when I spoke my first words to her then I knew why I saw Jesus Christ dipped under water.

She explained that I was cleaning myself with a white vest on because He wanted me to see what He did when He was alive. Days went by. I went down to the lobby and found Joyce once again. She looked at me and told me," Jennie, my spirit guide told me everything is ok." I gave her a big hug. Days went by, and I started to feel better. I began to feel myself again. As a matter of fact, as soon I felt myself again, I began to realize what I had thrown out. My telephone book that had everyone's addresses in. I realized that I couldn't remember what I had thrown out. I began to look around, and I was shocked because when I went to blow dry my hair.

I realized I had thrown out the hair dryer. I had thrown out so many things that I am still looking around wondering what else had I thrown out. I even threw out some of my clothes. I can't understand where all the power of energy came from? The energy I had was out of this world. I even threw out so many things that were very heavy. I know I didn't have anyone to help me. I understand some of my clothes were big, but some I wore around the house. When it was time to find a t-shirt with short sleeves, I only had two left and the rest were long sleeve that I wore to go outside in the cold.

I soon realized I had so much energy that I kept throwing stuff out all day long. At one point I locked myself out of my apartment at 1:30 in the morning. I called maintenance from housing to come and open the door for me. But they never came. I had to call my mother to open the door for me she gave me an extra key to my apartment. I did not tell my mom the truth about the day she came to give me the key, I told her I was throwing the trash out but did not tell her what kind of trash it was.

I cleaned my apartment so much that when I look around now it looked empty; I once had over two hundred angels I collected. I gave it all away. I even broke some while I was cleaning. I don't know why but I keep leaving the water running for four days straight. I can't explain why until one day everything changed. "I continued telling my mother the rest of the story." I started getting calmer, and I continue hearing my spiritual guide, and the rest of the voices but calmer. They were not screaming like they were doing previously. My spirit guide began talk normally. The voices calmed down by the end of August, but I kept hearing a voice or the angels talking with familiar voices, and they keep telling me not to be scared. That was the way how psychics talked to each other, but I could recognize all of the voices telling me to not be scared, everything will be fine. I did calm down because I trusted what they were saying for some reason.

Until I went to my friend Mayra's house because I had to tell her something. As soon as I got there, I soon realized the familiar voice I was hearing and trusting all this time. I realized something was not right. I didn't know why but I left Mayra's house so fast and once again I went home to cry my eyes out. When I was, hearing so many voices at that moment I said ok I am dead. I am in heaven, and I am hearing family's voices. Oh my God, I am in the sky, and He is in me. I was so scared out of my mind I still thought I could not think for myself. I thought, ok, they are choking my brain, I can't think. But then everything started to calm down in September 2007. I soon realized that I could not find all the poems and the notebook that I wrote all the predictions down in. I looked all over the house, but I realized I had also thrown them out too.

When everything started to calm down, I started to be myself again. One day I wanted to hear Gospel Music, I couldn't and I started to cry uncontrollably. As days went by I felt I grown up so much mentally, physically, emotionally. I felt at peace, so much peace in me. I felt very strange when I laughed. I felt like I should not be laughing. I even began to talk out more than before. I was a scaredy cat to give my opinion, but I felt so free like I don't have any problem in the world. I don't think of what I want for my future, I just don't think about tomorrow, just the day I'm in. I don't feel any worries, I have so much peace in me.

I am happy, and I thank God every day for that. I know the peacefulness I have inside me no one can take away. Even if anyone wants to argue I do not let anything bother me. I don't let anything get to me or get bothered by anything. That is a blessing, and I am happy for what God gave me. I have my health; I have my family and my friends. Why ask for more? It's a miracle to me, and I am thanking God again and all my angels each day for the experience I went through. I will never change it because I am happy with my life now more than ever. "As I continue telling my mother" I confessed to her that one time I did tell someone what was happening to me. To a family member, my cousin Leonor. That day I told her was when everyone was at my brother Ferdie's house having a cookout on August 25, 2007.

I found myself along with Leanor in the back yard. I told her a little, not all, about what was happening to me, that I started to hear my angels, and I could predict some of the family members' future. What I wrote down that they told me one was my cousin Edward Rivera and his girlfriend Monique, that they were having a baby.

Then I also told her that the Red Sox will win the World Series. I did trust Leanor because she was the oldest in the family, and she is a grandmother figure to all of us. My cousin Leonor is the last family member from my grandmother's generation. When Leonor looked at me, she smiled at me and said, "That's cool," then she told me some other family members had it too. That's right. Do I remember something that happened before everything a few months before all the angels started to speak to me? I was visiting Leonor at her house, and I was talking to her about that I could see sparkles, but I could not understand why, if or what did it mean. Or if I am reading people at that moment. Leonor said to me, "What do you see around me?" At that moment, I was surprised. I was going to say to her I have to relax to see if I could see your aura.

At that very moment, I could not say a word. To my surprise I started to see sparkles. It appeared out nowhere, and I called and told my mother, she was looking at some family picture on the wall in the hallway. She came back to the living room. I said, "Mom, check this out" and as I explained what happened, that exact moment when I looked at Leonor again" I said to her, "Wow, for some reason somehow what I get in my head a vision, and I think it is your father that came into my head."

While growing up we all called him Abuelo. In English it means grandfather. Everyone and even his cousins called him Abuelo but not by his real name, Jose Lourido. That day the only problem was I could not understand if they were trying to talk or what because I didn't hear anybody yet at that time. That is the reason I talked to her that day at the cookout. While everyone went inside, Leanor and I sat in the back yard and we talked a little that day about what happened to me.

I even told her I threw out all the book I wrote my predictions in. I even told her that I can remember every single word I wrote down. It was or still is like a cassette recording, everything but without a tape recorder. Leonor kept looking at me and said, "That is amazing, what happened to you." Then on September 14, 2007 my friend Katiria Montero called me, asking me if I could give her a ride to college. Even though she is much younger than me I was down for everything I had gone through. I began to tell her little by little, but I cried uncontrollably. She only heard me talk through my crying. A week went by. Katiria and I got together again. I told her more how I kept hearing the voices shouting, "He is coming, He is coming" and again I cried uncontrollably.

I told Katiria about me writing so many predictions down in a notebook. Katiria looked at me and told me that I had more guts than her. She even said she would have put herself in a psychiatric hospital, if she had kept hearing so many voices that way. I continued crying, and Katiria said, "Man, I never seen you cry at all." I looked at her, and I never cried so much in my life since this happened to me. That moment I started to laugh because Katiria told me, "Was Jesus Christ and the angels, did they open the faucet in you and let the water run and said this is the year that Jennie will start to cry?"

It made me laugh, and I agreed with her, one hundred percent. I told Katiria, "You are right on the money." I never cried so much in my entire life as I drove Katiria and I talked for a few more hours. I knew Katiria was younger than me, but I needed to get it out about how I saw Jesus Christ, Virgin of Guadalupe, all the angels and the Sacred Heart. I needed to tell my story to everyone, including my mother.

On September 20, 2007 I saw Lois Steward, who happened to be back from her vacation and I started to tell her everything that happened to me. I began telling her and again I began crying telling what I went through. Lois looked at me and said, "That's amazing. That was the Holy Spirit that you felt." I opened up to a few people that I felt I could trust. Days went by, and I saw buddy, a friend, from the building who at the time was in the lobby, and he asked me if the boy was still around. I told him yes. What do you think then? Buddy laughed and I began to tell him what happened to me. Before I could even finish telling him, he looked at me and said "You was possessed by Jesus himself?"

I looked at Buddy, surprised by what he said, because all this time I said I felt Jesus Christ in me. I did not dare say I was possessed by Him. Buddy looked at me and said, "That is a beautiful gift. You have seen Him, and all." I also talked to Dorothy Leger. As I sat down and talked to her and told her some of what had happened to me Dorothy looked at me and said, "You are here on this earth to do good and a great gift like that, you know you are chosen for something in this earth and you will do good." By the end of September, my mother knew a little about what happened to me and some of my neighbor's also kind of knew what happened to me.

I decided to see my neighbor Bertha to thank her for the support she gave me from the start. I knocked on her door, and she let me in. While I was talking to her; Bertha looked at me and told me, "I can't forget the day I went to your apartment in August." "When I saw, the image of the hand with the Virgin Mary in it and the hand vanished, I believe it came to me. When she said that I said, "Yes, it vanished as you got near the wall it was for you."

Then Bertha looked at me and said, "Do you remember what you told me when I was about to go home?" I looked at Bertha and said, "NO." I can't remember everything that happened in the month of August. Can you please tell me?" Bertha was ready to tell me. She said, "You can't remember what you said to me," and I looked at her and said, "No, please tell me. "I can't remember." Bertha looked at me and said, "Do you remember you had your water running in the kitchen, even in the bathroom?" I looked at her and said, "Yes, I do remember because I was mopping the floor.

And that was when I went to mop behind the door in my bedroom when I discovered the hand on the wall with the image of the Virgin Mary. That was the reason I came knocking on your door. I needed someone else to see if what I was seeing was correct." Then Bertha looked at me and told me, "Do you remember me and Paula when we were walking out the door?" I did remember that, Bertha said. "Do you remember what you told me at that moment."

As I waited to see what Bertha was about to tell me that will knock me over with shock, I began to cry. Bertha said, "While I walked toward the front door to go home I turned to you and asked you if I could turn off the faucet in the bathroom and you told me no. Because you said 'He told you to do it.' 'He told me to do it' over and over." I was so shocked when Bertha finished telling me. As I heard what Bertha told me my blood drained out of me. Chills ran down my spine. I put my hand on my mouth and began to cry and I looked at her so surprised and told her, "I wish I could remember that. But what I gone through so much I can't remember some of the events that happened in the month of August it was a blur.

Even though August was all "'Miracles,'" it was not easy to go through it. But I would not change it for the world." When I finished talking to Bertha, I thanked her for everything and hugged her for telling me what I had said that fateful day. I even remembered that day in August. I remember when my Aunt Maria was in my mother's bedroom, and she told me "don't change your ways." My Aunt happened to notice something different with me and told me not to change my ways. "I asked her what she meant by that?" My aunt explained to me, "Don't stop laughing and don't stop having fun. You are a great person, and you have a great heart. You are a person that loves to smile and likes to have fun." But while I sat there hearing her telling me this my mind wandered off. I was still hearing her telling me things.

I was thinking to it was too late but she kept talking to me and I kept saying it is too late over and over. My life is changed, and I'm feeling completely different, a new person. Then one day I went to Mayra's house, and I did not know how to begin by telling her everything that happened to me. I did know she sent me to her mother Edelmira. I did explain to Mayra that her mother helped me, and she even helped me understand what was happening to me.

While I was talking to Mayra, I also found out something that happened that I didn't know about. While we spoke about what happened in August, Mayra stopped me and said the day I came over she was surprised because it was 8 o'clock. And when her husband Chino opened the door and told her that it was me, she was surprised because I don't come late to her house unless it was a party. Besides I even followed her around the house, and that was not like me, and beside I left fast.

That is when I responded, "I did tell you I had to go, but I did not tell you why I left that fast. Besides I didn't know what time it was." Mayra also told me she got so worried about me because the of way I acted; she told her daughter Katiria and Chino something is so wrong with Jennie, and she is acting weird. Marya also told me she wanted to call me that night, but she got so busy with the kids that she forgot to call me. At that moment, I told her everything and began to cry, explaining to her that the reason I came to see her. The first time I was so scared because I wanted someone to know what was going on and maybe help me. I did not understand why I saw double I was seeing through someone else's eyes. I even told Mayra I was hearing so many angels shouting, "He is coming!" I explained "That's when you sent me to your mother to help me, and I am happy you did.

When I came to talk to you, I was still hearing the angels' voices but at the time they were familiar voices. To calm me down the angels kept talking, telling me not to be scared when I came to see you, I did not know what time it was. I lost track of time." When I left as fast as I came, it was because I realized that the familiar voices, I heard were not who I thought it was. At that moment, I thought I really was crazy. I went home to cry as I kept explaining to Mayra that I was glad I had finally told her the truth. On January 7, 2008 I went to my mother's house at twelve in the afternoon.
As I walked in, I saw my mom in the kitchen with her brother Edward and his wife Maria. As I sat down my mother told me, "I need to tell you something." I looked at her and asked her, "What you need to tell me?" My mother looked at me and told me that at 7:45 a.m.

She was taking her grandkids to school. When she told her grandson, Kyle who was in the front seat of the car that she could not see, that the sun, was blinding her. She asked Kyle to put the car visor down. At that exact moment she asked Kyle to stop. "Do you see what I am seeing, Kyle?" He told my mother yes. They both had seen the sun changing. My mother started to describe the sun. It was an aura as she called it. Different colors around the sun and then like something covered the sun. Like the moon went over it, and I could see where I was going, the only thing I didn't see was Jesus Christ. When my mother told me about the sun changing, I started to cry inconsolably again because that moment my mom told her brother Edward, "I believe God showed me the sun for me to believe my daughter."

I felt a relief that my mother finally believed me. Three days later I went over to, my Aunt Carmelina's house. As we talked for a while we started to talk about religion. When I started to tell her, what happened to me back in August as I could not tell all the story. I couldn't as I was crying inconsolably. My mom had to finish the story and also told her something like that happened to her on January 7, 2008. I began getting used to hearing the angels talking to me. I never thought of asking my spirit guide to tell me why they used familiar voices, why are they shouting at me. I got so scared; I didn't know what was happening. I was panicked and scared, and that's why I began to go to church every day. Thinking back and writing this part I feel like crying because all that time I was thinking for myself. I thought the angels, or as I called them at the time the voices, were choking my brain and all the time I was hearing my spirit guide telling me, "You are thinking for yourself, don't worry, don't be afraid," the more I cried

Still looking for reasons

I needed to know why this was happening, to me I kept looking for an explanation why did I see Jesus Christ. The more I looked for answers I decided to call Reverend Simon. He is a medium in Boston, Massachusetts and asked him if I could see him but that was in the month of September and for some reason I did not get a chance to see him, every time I was ready to see him something happened and he or I had to cancel.

But the day finally came that I got to see him. It was the month of January 3, 2008 when I got to his office. I sat down in front of him, and he began to read me. He told me that I indeed had seen Jesus and that Jesus indeed came toward me and I was feeling His presence, and the hand of Jesus was showing me I was going the right way. When the reverend said that I began to cry then I asked him why the voices were screaming at me. He explained that the angels wanted me to know that Jesus was coming. I answered to the Reverend, "Why didn't they say that instead of shouting at me? "He is coming, He is coming" so many times." The Reverend looked at me and said, "If they would have told you that you were going to see Jesus Christ would you have believed them?" That moment I sat back and my answer was "NO!" I would never have believed that I was going to see Jesus Christ, especially when I am still alive. Then the most important question I needed to ask, "Why do the angels use familiar voices after they stop screaming?" The Reverend said, "They wanted you to realize they were here not to harm you but to help you. And showing you things, and that was the only way for you to realize that you will be seeing the future and helping people in the future."

He also explained that sometimes the angels do mistakes by not using their voices. And by using people you know that way you don't get scared and then the Reverend looked at me and asked me, "Was you scared?" I looked at him with tearful eyes and answered "YEAH!" I was scared, very terrified. I was so scared it was too many voices all at once. To a point I thought I was a million miles away in the future. I thought I was in the sky hearing my family and friends saying things. The Reverend told me that the angels didn't want me to get scared that "bad."

In one moment into the conversation I said "ghost" when the Reverend started to laugh and said, "Jennie, the angels don't like it when you call them ghosts, they are angels and spirit." I looked at him so surprised and said they don't like that I call them "ghost" with all I went through. They are complaining that I call them "ghost," sure, that is easy for them to say, they are not the one that was crying and scared half to death. Then the Reverend was almost finished reading me he looked at me and said, "You know there is a story line out of this." At that moment, I realized after I left his office that I also wrote it in one of my predictions. I remember writing in a notebook that I was writing a book, and I would be writing about me and my family and friends.

What was happening to me? So here I am back on track, I am actually shocked that I am writing this book and happy at the same time. While predictions I wrote started to come true, another prediction that came true was my cousin Edward Rivera and his girlfriend Monique Ocasio were having a baby. I told this prediction about my cousin and his girlfriend to my mother but never got a chance to tell anyone else.

It is funny because I was telling my mother about the prediction that I wrote about my cousin Edward Rivera and Monique Ocasio were going to have a baby but while I was telling my mother, I thought where it will be further into the future. Then a couple of days went by when my mother told me about her dream that she had about someone being pregnant. When my mother told me that, I smiled and said maybe someone is pregnant but we didn't think anything of it. The next day my Aunt Carmelina was, talking to her sister Nellie and me when she mentioned that she had a dream about someone being pregnant. I laughed and said, "Ok, then someone for sure is pregnant?"

But to my surprise my mother Nellie called me on January 26, 2008 to tell me the good news about my cousin Edward, and Monique; they were expecting a baby. At the time she was four months along. Did I not think that the predictions I wrote was for this year? I thought maybe for the year 2015 and beyond. I decided not to write down some of the predictions, yet one reason is that I am new at this.

The second reason is some of the predictions I do know who and I'm thinking if I say something and it doesn't happen, what are people are going to say? That I am a liar. But then I came to understand after thinking about it I really don't care what people will say anymore. I wrote this book because I had to tell my story. And if one of my predictions is right, in 2008 the Red Sox will win that is the only hint I give at this moment in time. Now if I am wrong then I was right to keep the rest of my predictions to myself. Besides, I made a promise to Jesus Christ when the time is right, I will speak up and tell everyone all the predictions, but for now I keep it to myself.

As the day's went by I became more curious than I already was, I needed some answers to what was happening to me, I needed to understand and as human as I am. I know that there are also curious people in the world who look for answers like I do. I guess I needed to know more about the spiritual world. Why did I see the boy, then year's later I see Jesus Christ and why did I feel His presence in me? Besides, I understand that, what I was going through was something so wonderful but at the same time because I was alone, I was so scared. That is the reason I write this book: to help each other. And if there is anyone that needs my help in anyway and by writing this book someone out there like yourself who is reading this needed some explanations or someone to believe you. "You are not alone and you might not be crazy."

I could be the one person who could understand what you are going through. I was so scared from everything that happened to me I needed to get more answers for my question. I couldn't understand why so many miracles keep surrounding me? I know some people just take it as it is and keep going with their life, but I need answers. I know I did tell some of the few miracles that happened to me to a few close friends, and family member's, explaining to them what I saw. When I began to cry more was when I saw Jesus Christ, Angels, and the Virgin of Guadalupe. Some people don't know who the Virgin of Guadalupe is, she is the Virgin from Mexico. I knew of her, but I didn't think I would see her. Matter of fact, I would not ever expect to see any miracles in my life, not like the way I saw it. I saw the sun change in front of me and even seeing the moon years ago; I still don't know why the moon looked like it was on the ground?

Learning about Mediums and Psychics

I don't blame anyone if they search for answers. As I have done myself, and like I said I was like a kid, whatever I see I need to know why and how come. I used to look at the world different but now I look at the world with honor and respect. I am grateful that people will get to know who I am and what I went through. The one reason I really wanted to tell my story is like I said before maybe someone out there may have gone through the same thing. And maybe they got more scared than I did. Then maybe I could help them out even by writing this story, I could have the answers to some of their questions. "GOD BLESS" anyone who did go through this experience because it is hard to go through it alone. I can't explain this spiritual journey, even though I call it a gift. Even though it is free, when you get it there, there is no one to ask how it works. I know it doesn't come with instructions, but it is hard to understand.

That is if you have never seen anyone else go through it, or experience the spiritual world. Like when I saw the boy for the first time, I decided to learn more about the spiritual world. I decided to start reading different psychic books like Sylvia Brown, Rosemary Altea, Doreen Virtue and John Edwards. The one I connected the most was with Doreen Virtue. She writes about angels, and I also read a few other books. But reading, I never saw anyone in any of their book's having experienced similar events as me. I know I have heard or have seen people who have experienced miracles. Even if they are in different religions. Even sometimes in each religion there is someone who had spiritual experience or saw or heard their own spiritual guide.

Some people keep it quiet to themselves because sometimes their family is too fast to judge and they afraid of what they should say to them or to anyone for that matter. That is the reason I am speaking out because I don't have anything to be ashamed of. I am happy and at peace that God gave me a present; seeing Him is a beautiful gift. While I go through this wonderful journey, I keep getting surprises. One day I was talking to a friend. I was telling her about what happened to me and what I was writing. While I was talking to her, I noticed she kept saying, "I SEE THAT." At first, I didn't think anything of it, as I was busy crying, but soon. I realized after she kept repeating it, "I SEE THAT."

I looked at her and finally asked her why do you keep saying, "I SEE THAT" every time I tell you what happened to me. She finally told me that she got picture clips like a little video. That's the way her spirituality worked and that's how she sees things. That is when I knew! What I was writing was true, by her acknowledgment by what she was seen telling me it was true. That's when I realized that I had to write my book. It gave me more realization that this was the moment to tell my story to the world. A month later I remember the Reverend also told me that sometimes mediums or psychic people can say names and some of them can't.

I wanted to know my spirit guide's name; even though I keep hearing her telling me her name I refuse to believe her. I thought ok, she reading my mind since I heard her name once before. So, I decided to call Jacki Joy to ask her if she could tell me my spirit guide's name. I did keep hearing my guide telling me her name, but I was not trusting anyone yet with everything I went through.

When I called Jacki, we talked for a little while. I could not come out asking her so fast. Besides, I didn't want to tell her the real reason, I was calling her. We talked on the phone for a while. And then I did finally ask her if she could tell me what was my spirit guide's name. But before I could even finish saying spirit, Jacki told me her name was Theresa. I was shocked because this was the same lady was talked to me back when my family and I took our vacation to Virginia. I also thanked Jacki Joy for all the support she helps me with, I also thanked Jesus Christ for having her on this earth and letting me get to know her.

In March 2008 I went to pick up a family, friend and when she got in my car, she said, "I got to tell you something." She told me that she saw a lady behind me. I looked at her surprised. I asked her what the lady looked like. She said curly blond hair and she wore an old-fashioned dress. A I was hearing her describe the lady to me. I started to hear my spirit guide telling me: **"THAT IS ME! THAT IS ME!"** My friend even told me she had seen her two other times when she was going to get in my car. Then I decided to ask my friend if she could tell me more. I asked her what year the guide was born. She told me around the "1700s" and when she said that I was glad because my spirit guide did tell me months before that she was from the 1700s.

Like always I had a hard time believing her in the beginning. Months went by and in January, I saw my friend Hollis. I needed to talk to her and ask her where she got the saint statue, she had given me for Christmas. I told her I had broken it when I was cleaning my house back in August. I felt so bad because I liked my statues. When I approached her and told her, I needed to tell her about what happened to me.

Hollis saw me crying for the first time. As a matter of fact, my family and friends always said I didn't have a heart because I never cried. When I began to tell Hollis everything, I began to cry. I was shaking like a leaf. I explained everything to her; I even want to thank Hollis for being a good friend. I can't forget my family member who I talked to. It was September 1, 2007, I never will forget his words, and I can't recall if I called him or he called me. My cousin Ariel and me were talking for a while. When I told him what happened to me, his words were shocking to me. He said, "Jennie, you know there is a saying Jesus walks beside you." I said, "Yes" "Well, He carried you all that month of August." When he told me that I asked him to repeat it. He responded by you telling me, you felt Him in you, then He carried you. I was overwhelmed that my cousin Ariel had that powerful word of wisdom, besides he calmed me down from crying. I thanked him and hung up the phone. I continued to learn from each person that is a psychic or mediums who has had their spiritual experience longer than I have. Even learning from different mediums by reading their book's I thank God for people who write book's. By reading the spiritual books I have to say it did help me understand a little more about how spiritualty works. Let me say whoever becomes a psychic or a medium, or like I call myself a spiritual reader, it's not easy. I did learn the hard way running from my house in the middle of the night. It was not easy, but I got used to it. By seeing so many miracles, it was wonderful. Now that I know the facts.

After what I went through in August that is another reason, I needed to learn to get used to hearing my spirit guide and understanding how this works, It's no easy task. It does change your life by each passing day. I got used to hear the spirit guide speak to me. Writing this story is a big challenge but it is not like back in the 1700 or the 1800 when you had to hide their secrets. Because you get hanged or burned at the stake and because people were more ashamed of it. Even family members scared the heck out of you by saying that you were crazy or have evil inside you and many more things. Now in 2008 people are more open minded. Nowadays you have TV shows like "The Ghost Whispers" "Medium," "Supernatural," "Montel Williams" that has a guest Sylvia Brown on his show. Even TV specials like John Edwards and similar shows like "Dead Zone," "Ghost Hunters and it's a lot more but I ran out of pages. And especially the Spanish channels. Sometimes they have a show about people who have their gift. You can see the show taps the people who look for ghosts nowadays. It is more open now than back in the days when my great-great grandmother Eliza Muñez or her daughter Conchita were around. I have to repeat it because it was amazing for me. I would never forget when I saw the sun change. I could even look straight at the sun the entire month of August. But after August, I try to look at the sun, and it is so bright, that I can't even look up at it.

Looking back, I would never have thought that I would have gone through that experience. I did suffer a lot, but I have to admit I did choose to keep it to myself. I didn't want my loved ones to see me hurting. I did not know how to explain that I was hearing people screaming. What could I have said if I didn't know what was going on myself? This is why I decided to keep it to myself and still I thank God every day for the experience even if I got so panicked and thought they stole my brain. I learned that each day is a gift of life and what happened to me and each day that passes is a wonderful experience that I will never want to change in my life. In all of this, I have to admit I had not talked to my guide at this time at all but everything changed one day.

First words with a Spirit Guide

One day I was at the store, and I was alone I was buying a shirt. When I finished paying, I left the store. But I started to hear the spirit guide telling me, "Don't leave the shopping cart in the middle of the aisles." I thought, why are they telling me this not to leave the shopping cart in the middle of the aisles of the store. I found it strange, but I started to go out the door, and again I heard my guide tell me, "Don't leave the shopping cart in the middle of the aisles." I kept thinking why is it wrong to leave the shopping cart in the middle of the store? Everyone else does it. That was my thought, but I did not ask my spirit guide why are you are telling me this?

When I got next to my car, I soon realized that I had the bag where I bought my shirt, but I forgot my purse in the shopping cart in the middle of the aisles. I ran and got the shopping cart, and I got my purse back after I left the store. I decided to ask my spirit guide for the first time why you didn't tell me it was my purse and kept saying shopping cart; the only answer I got was, "I can't tell you everything." I was surprised with the answer. Then on January 30, 2008 I was at my house, and I happened to lose my earring and I looked everywhere for it. I looked in the bathtub because I thought I lost it there; I had taken a shower an hour before.

Then I looked under the pillow. I went back in the bathroom to see if I saw it after an hour or two of looking. I finally gave up and for the first time. I talked to my spirit guide and asked her, "Can you please tell me where my earring is?" Her answer was, "Inside your bra." She repeated it twice.

I can't say if I asked her if she said bra, but she said loud and clear, "Inside your bra." To my surprise I looked inside my shirt; it was inside my bra. I laughed with a surprise on my face, and I did thank my spiritual guide for helping me out. On February 2008, I kept hearing my spirit guide tell me, "You are going to get "dizzy." But I did not ask why, I just wondered why I will get "dizzy." I didn't feel any different, so I never asked. But then a few days later I went to a funeral to pay my last respects to a family member.

When I went to the bathroom, I was washing my hands when I saw the niece of the deceased family member. We began talking and, in that moment, she looked at me and said, "I am dizzy." I looked surprised and laughed because it was not me, but the lady that was going to say she was dizzy. A week went by and I was at home, and once again I heard my spirit guide tell me, "You have an ear infection." She repeated it three time. Like before, I thought I don't feel any pain, I don't feel any problem with my ears. Then I went to my mother's house. When I opened the door and saw my niece Dede walking toward me the first words out of her mouth were, "Auntie Jennie, I got an ear infection." I did get a kick out of it because I was not expecting that.

I know Jesus Christ gave me this spiritual journey for a reason but for me this is a great honor to have it, and that's my opinion. Now I know I need to help people with it. It will also be a great honor to work with God and His white light. I know my spiritual guide speaks to me and sometimes I don't answer her back or ask her what something means. While each day passes the spirit, guide keep explaining things to me. As days and months go by sometimes, I did write down what they said.

But I didn't ask any questions Each day I keep learning one step at a time, besides I leave it in "Jesus Christ's hands." Looking back, I never imagined I'd be going through this spiritual experience as wonderful as it was. I know I did suffer a lot, but I had a choice to tell someone or keep it to myself, besides like I said before I didn't want for my family to see me hurting. How could I explain that I was hearing the voices screaming at me "HE IS COMING," what could I have said if I didn't know myself what was coming at that time. Besides how could I go and tell my mother something like that. As nervous as she is would have given her a heart attack. That is one reason I chose to keep it to myself. Not let anyone else suffer like I was at the time, and still I thank God every day for the experience even if I got so panicked and scared. Whatever my future holds for me I will leave it in the hands of Jesus. I am so honored and proud He came to me. I thought I was the only one seeing things in my family until one day my cousin Laura told me her experience.

Laura told me her experience

On February 2008 my mother's first cousin Laura came for a visit from Puerto Rico. It had been 28 years since she left Boston. She came to visit her sister in law Brianca but when Brianca sent for her sister in law, Brianca ended up in the hospital. So, Laura stayed with my mother for two weeks. During Laura's stay, I found out a little bit more about my great-great grandmother Eliza Muñez. I kept asking around to find out what kind of a spiritual gift Eliza Muñez had. While Laura was here, she told me that Eliza was a healer, she would take herbs to heal people. I wonder if she could hear her spiritual guide or if her daughter Conchita had her spiritual guide.

I wish my grandmother Blanca could have been able to tell me more, but she could not at the time of her sickness. Laura told me she also had a religious experience happen to her. She started explaining that she went to the church of the Seven Day Adventists. While the minister was preaching, she saw a white dove fly over her and vanish. She told me she looked around to see if anyone else saw it. But no one else saw anything, she didn't see anyone looking for a white dove. She continued to hear her minister preaching. Laura saw the white dove again. This time it flew over toward the minister and vanished, and at that exact moment she saw a lot of light's surrounding him. She described that there were so many beautiful colors that she had never seen before. When I was hearing her story, I got goose bumps. When she described the white dove going over to her minister that's when I told her that when she saw the colors around him it was his aura what she saw. We kept talking little bit longer.

I told her I know how she felt seeing the colors. There are no words to describe the feeling the colors give and the colors are so different from the colors we see every day. Hearing this story, I wanted to find out more. Who else had this spiritual gift in my family? The only way to find out something is when we have family gatherings and some of the family members sometimes talk about ghost stories. And what they had experienced themselves when they were younger, but to hear a story and experience it myself now that was a different story. What happened to me was a gift from God. I know a lot of people will have their opinion. I understand that but I know some of you will be judged but until people walk in my shoes and experience what I went through they shouldn't be judging that quickly. Like I said before I understand each spiritual gift is different even though each person who senses things or sees a ghost or can read people, any kind of spirituality is different.

While I kept myself busy learning by reading different psychic books, I also learned from some of my family member like Lillian, Marie, Anthony, Mildred, and Yamir, even though their gifts are totally different from mine. Even the people in the spiritual group called metaphysical. I do keep learning and experiencing new things and I have learned so far that there are mental and physical challenges but no matter what I do I work with a white light and only the white light. I understand that my journey has just begun. And no matter what direction I take I know that Jesus Christ is holding my hands and is walking with me each step of the way. Sometimes you get an uneasy feeling you can't explain. That has happened to me a couple of time in my life, but this day I will never forget.

Uneasy Feeling

On February 29, 2008 I was in my apartment concentrating on writing my book. My mother called me and asked me if I wanted to go to my cousin Blanch's house that weekend. I told her that I could not because I had already taken three days off from working on my book. Then on March 2, 2008 I was working on my book, I started to wonder if I should go to Blanch's house. That's when I heard my spirit guide tell me go out, you need to go. You have been staying in your house for a long time. As I stood my ground I still didn't want to go. I wanted to keep working on my book, but. I kept getting an uneasy feeling that I needed to go.

I know my mother was going with her brother Edward and his wife Maria but in the last second, I decided to go. The reason I decided to go was if they talked about something from the past and it was good, I could put it in the book. I was trying to know more about Eliza Muñez and her daughter Conchita and see if I could get more pictures for my book and second for some reason, I kept getting the feeling that I needed to go. So, at the last minute I went to my mother's house. When my mother saw me and realized I was going, she told her brother Edward that she will go in my car with our cousin Laura.

While my uncle went with his wife Maria and their granddaughter Daisy and my niece, Dede went with him. While we were driving to Boston my mother and our cousin Laura were listening religious music. After a while, we started to talk and when I happened to look in the rear-view mirror to see if my Uncle Edward was still behind me, I noticed my uncle's car was smoking.

I saw dark smoke coming from the engine. When we were pulling out from the highway to the next exit, we stopped in a parking lot. I heard my spirit guide say to me, "This is the reason you had to come, to make sure everyone was safe." The car caught on fire everyone got in my car while we were only 20 minutes away from Blanch's house. They all got in my little Pontiac Grand Am. Everyone was so scared. What had happened to the car? I told my mother what my spirit guide Theresa had told me. My mother told the family later on it was shocking that in the last second Jennie decided to come, since she had wanted to stay home and work on the book. Even though something keeps pushing me to go even if it was my spirit guide or my intuition, I thanked God. I was so positive that I was there to help my family out. Later we found out that the car did not burn all the way but was put out quickly. Where the fire started was next to the right front tire. Days went by and I got a surprise I was not expecting because after what I went through 2007 and cleaned my house and throwing stuff away, I never thought I would get anything back.

What I went through

On March 2008, I was coming home from the store when I got off the elevator with my neighbor Paula. When she told me to follow her into her apartment I did and she explained to me that she knew how much I had suffered back in the month of August 2007. That I had left some of my collection of angels on the bench for the people of the building to have. I told her I did not remember which bench I left the angels on. Paula told me the reason I asked you to follow me was to give you this box. When I looked in the box, I was shocked. She was returning one of my angels back. In my opinion I never thought I would ever see any of the collection of angels again. It was nice of her to give me the angel back. I did tell her she should keep it, but Paula said no I knew what you went through, and I wanted you to have it.

After having this experience, so many things since the first time it all started, I will never take life for granted, I love my life, and I love every minute of each day. I am so blessed for having experiences. As many miracles that I witness and to have this spiritual gift. I still don't call myself a psychic or a medium, but I know whatever comes my way. I know I could handle anything with grace. God willing. While I sit here writing this book, I think back when I saw the boy that appeared to me that August 2000 until now 2008. I understand that what happened to me with so many miracles surrounding me and to experience something so wonderful like seeing Jesus. To experience that first hand and feel His presence in me was overwhelming.

Especially seeing Him come toward me with His hands wide open and then seeing the Virgin of Guadalupe, the sacred heart and to see so many angels, it is so amazing to talking about. It still feels unreal, but I know a true "MIRACLE." I can't forget the hand on the wall with the Virgin Mary in the middle of the hand behind my bedroom door. This was an amazing experience. The entire month of August of 2007. I wondered if the moon that I saw was the one from August 1995, Should I include this as a miracle? But in all the searching I did I realized that the moon might not be paranormal. And was if that experience I had back when I lived in my sister law Marie's grandparents' house for me to learn or was it preparing me for what was to come in 2007 and the voice of the men, I heard the first time in the motor home?

I didn't let him say what he needed to tell me. Was he trying to prepare me too? And so many times I had gone to bed I kept hearing a lady's voice trying to say something to me and I dismissed it. What if she was trying to prepare me for the future? Or the last voice I heard saying you can do it. Were they trying to tell me something or are they trying to prepare me for all that I went through? "If I am right then it didn't work that well because nothing prepares you for such a beautiful experience's no matter if you get scared or not." I started thinking, and I wondered if I was already feeling my guide telling me something or not because in the year 2005 my mother went into a store, and I waited in the car.

I mentioned to my nephew Kyle, who was in the car with me that I needed some Chap stick. I wondered if my mother could get me some. Kyle offered to go in the store and tell my mother to get me Chap stick, but I told him no it was ok. When my mother came out of the store, she got in the car and said to me, "Jennie, here I got you Chap stick." I looked at my nephew Kyle and looked at my mother and said, "I just told Kyle I wanted to get Chap stick." I was shocked and amazed that I thought of something, and I got it. What happened next would shock me even more. One day I had a cold, I was coughing and I wanted to get some cough medicine. I kept thinking I would like to get a honey medicine and for two straight days I kept wondering if the store sells the honey cough medicine. When I was with my mother, she decided to go into a drug store I stayed in the car. While waiting in the car, I keep thinking about the medicine and wondering if I had asked my mother if she could find the honey medicine, but I never did ask her. But when she got out of the drug store, she told me, "Here, I got you this medicine." When I opened the bag to my surprise, it was the honey cough medicine.

I was amazed that she got it without me telling her the kind of medicine I wanted or that I wanted some medicine at all. Amazing as, it is, I wondered what kind of connection I had. Was it with the thought or do I have a connection with my mother's vibes? Or could it be all together at the same time? Or was I getting messages from my guide without me knowing? Or are they preparing me for a lot more? I guess I have to find out more on my own as each day passes. I think of two scenarios when my great great-great grandmother Eliza was in the era 1800's era. When no one wanted to be an outcast even back then, parents did tell their children that they were evil to have a supernatural experience. I guess it was a hard time for Eliza and her daughter Conchita having the spiritual gift. Even for Conchita it was not safe in the 1900's, no one wanted to be pointed out as a witch that saw spirits. I guess it was hard for them in those days. As I kept searching,

I found some information from the family that Eliza Muñez was a spiritual healer and used herbs to help people out. It's cool to know that she knew about herbs, it's interesting, and I wonder how she knew how to use the herbs on people. I realized that this spirituality or as I call it spiritual gift did skip generations because it jumped my mother's generation, and it passed to me and a few others. I have to think what will happen to the younger generation like my nieces and nephews or cousins. Could it skip the generation like it did with my mother's generation? Only time would tell and only God knows the answer to that. This spirituality is hard to deal with when you are alone. I believe it is much easier when your family or friends support you. Nowadays more people are open to the spiritual world believing in psychic's or mediums. We still have people in the world who are nonbelievers and some that don't even believe in Jesus Christ. And there are people who like to do name calling, they like to offend by calling someone a witch, and it's even more cruel if you don't know the person in the first place.

Why the name calling? Until that person walks in the other person's shoes, then you will never know what the other person went through and by calling them cruel names the people always will be separate between nonbeliever and religion. I am Catholic, and I am proud that what happens to me and it is a miracle. People can believe whatever they like. People have got their own opinions, I also understand we all come with different religions, and I am not judging anyone for their beliefs. I want to thank Jesus every day for the gift He has given me. I do feel happiness, peace and, love in me, physically, and mentally.

I do feel like I don't have a weight on my shoulders. I can't explain it but it is amazing. I feel free. And with all that feeling what more can I ask for I know now that my journey has just begun, and it's changing me for the better. What happened to me was more than a miracle, it was a blessing. I am happy and with each day that passes I will accept this "GIFT" that JESUS gave me with His help, of course. Without Him nothing is possible. I have to say I did learn to take one day at a time, and I don't rush life, I just learn how it comes and goes one hour at a time. It's the greatest gift. I say to those who are reading this book look around and see where you are going because at the end of the day you are still standing in the same spot with the same problems. Let the problems go and put it in "GOD's" hands and let Him lead the way. Sit down and pray, and everything will come in time. Don't rush it. Jesus never gives you anything you can't handle. You can see your life will get better each day no matter how rough it gets. You can handle it, with prayers and God's help. Just keep your head up, believe in yourself and keep your faith strong. I know it's hard but life is not easy, it's just a learning experience.

You need to keep going if you know what you want in your future. You will have the peace you are looking for. It takes time to get there, don't rush it. I have to say many predictions that people had told me have come true. Like the day, I asked my sister in law, Marie, to read me. When I asked her if I should move to a building, I was thinking about what she told me. I would be arguing with someone in the building, I thought then, why move? But when Marie read me, she did not know how to explain with who or when will the arguing happen. Marie did the reading in 2003.

And I didn't move thinking I am arguing with someone in the other building. Not knowing in 2005 the argument did happen and it was with two of the people in my building. I had nothing against them, they got into my private life, and we got into an argument. Marie's prediction came true.

I believe she was not used to doing readings or explaining what she gets in her readings. Like she said when I asked if I should move and she saw that I was arguing with someone, my thought was why move then, since if I had moved or not the argument still would have happened. Whether it is in your life predictions or not, you still pick out your life charts before you're born.

A Different outlook

I was sitting outside my building on April 17, 2008, and it was 70 degrees. I looked around and saw the beauty of the world around me, and I came to the realization I was so happy with who I had become. I was so blessed with a gift that Jesus gave me. I was even filling so rich at this very moment in my life. I look at the beauty beyond anyone's imagination. Years ago, I used to worry if I could not make it somewhere. Where I had to be, I got upset. I did learn from two different people, my friend's Mayra and my other friend Hollis. When I started to hang out with them, they both got my attention, and they both told me one day, "If you did not get to a place there is a reason for that."

I asked them what they meant by that. They both told me to think about it. What happened if you are in a rush and an accident occurred? Or you are meant to be late, or you never get there at all. Or something happened you could not make it at all. Sometimes God had another purpose for you not to being there. Those few words stuck with me like glue. That's why I don't get mad or upset if I get somewhere late or don't get there at all. I'm surely a believer before we are born that we are given a chart with things we need to learn to do.

While we are living our lives, we keep going and everything we do, we check things off as we learn from it. I believe when everything is all done, that's when Jesus Christ calls us home. Sometimes we get sidetracked and do things we might regret. But the pain and suffering that we sometimes put ourselves through is also on our chart which we have to learn each step of the way.

Jesus Christ is with us through good times. He is even there through the bad times. Jesus is always there to help us get back on track. We have many obstacles that we all agree before we are born to put in our paths. With all that Jesus Christ knows, we can overcome them, and we will get stronger for the next obstacle. Some people start great and then it starts getting tough on them, then what they do is quit. Some people tell their kids or other people that they will never make it that they are not good enough to do what they want. Then they quit because they are so easily influenced by what other people say. Some people get angry or decide to hurt you but in the end it is up to you to get to your goals.

What you didn't know is that those people are just a small obstacle placed in your path. Just remember quitting is not an option. Those people who influenced you and tell you that you're not good enough. Remember don't let that stop you. Sometimes you need to get angry, take that anger and energy and keep going. Twenty percent do more in their life than anyone expected you to do. It will be your choice if you hear the person that told you that you will not amount to anything. Take a look who is around you and see who is around to teach you a valuable lesson.

Life is about learning and having an outlook in life. Its takes time to learn. Even complaining and worrying about not having any money or complaining about how you are going to pay the bills. Stop worrying and stop complaining and start focusing on what you want in life and have faith, and you will see that everything will fall into place, and everything will work out. In my opinion if you can do anything you want in life sometimes people want to have the cake and eat it too.

It takes a long time to eat the cake, but the longer you wait, the better the cake will taste.

Now that is my opinion and with the faith I have, it surely works for me. As I said before with the help of Jesus Christ of course. Have faith in yourself, sit down and talk to Jesus Christ like you are talking to a friend. Don't sit there and say oh I can't, I don't know what to say, or I've got to go out I don't have time, even saying I am too busy doing things. If you have time for parties or watching TV or just lying in bed, then you can take 20 minutes of your life and talk to Jesus. He will hear you out. It doesn't matter how you do it. You speak without opening your mouth, just thinking about it He still hears you or screaming out loud. He does hear your prayers day or night; Jesus will answer you in His way. You will get your answer. It could be in your dreams or a sign. You just have to be aware of it, or it could be someone is talking to you and by the conversation you get the answer you are looking for; it will be in the conversation. Jesus Christ makes sure He gives you the message you are looking for and it will come to you loud and clear. You'll be very surprised where your answer will come from. Everyone has a different look in life but even understand that sometimes we are so busy that Jesus is knocking on everyone's door trying to support your daily life. One day I was talking to a complete stranger, and he asked me why Jesus left him. I responded telling him, "He never left you." You are the one who left Him, you could be so busy with your life, just talk to Him, and He will hear you out." Where this happened was in a chat room. A few days later his chat room name showed up again asking me if I was the person, he talked to few days ago.

I told him yes, it was me. I found out it was not the same man who I talked to the first time.

It was a relative trying to locate me because this person left me a note thanking me because I helped him believe in Jesus again, his family found the guy dead three days later with the Bible in his hand.

I have to say it happened around 2004 or 2005 while I was in the chat room. He went to my website and came back to the chat room. I was still in the chat room, he asked me later if he could talk to me. We began to talk. I realized later we had a conversation for three hours. It was all about religion. He did tell me he was sick, but I did not know how bad it was. I have to say it shocked me that someone in his family looked for a complete stranger like me, to thank me with a letter he left behind. I know it was a chat room, but he did sign my guest book, and I will never forget, because he wrote thanks for saving him, but I never kept his name. Not because I didn't want to, but because my website at the time got full. And I needed more space. When his family member spoke to me, I did tell them he signed my guest book. And I guess he was so overwhelming for that person he or she got off the chat room and the last words were, "I can't take this" and left. Years later I still think about it.

No matter if it could have been true or not, even if that person could have been a scammer by pulling my leg. I still feel I did help someone that needed to talk to somebody. I tell this story to people because it changed something in me. And it was not about his death or because he was just a teenager. Because the only two time we talked he kept saying, he found God.

In that few days we talked and also how he left earth in peace. No matter if it was true or not, besides his chat room name never came back up, and I kept his name in the chat room for two years. I thank God for each day for allowing me to help a person who needed help like this person did. If it happened for real or if it was a joke I never truly knew, but in my opinion I'm glad I helped him out if it was true.

I understand people do things in a chat room to fool people, but I felt this was true, besides I had my website for over six years. I didn't take it down, it got canceled on me. To my surprise my website became religious and also to my surprise a lot of people liked my site and signed it. Only a few people were scared away from it. My site was not meant to be religious, it just happened and hopefully I will try to do another website as soon as possible.

Religion

I'm writing something I think about often. I try not offend anyone on this subject. The reason I say this is because people nowadays get offended by anything that has to do with religion. I understand that there are a lot of different religions in the world. One day I happened to be walking, and I passed this man and he said to me, "smiling, "God loves you." It was a blessing to hear that but at the same time I was shocked because this person was a complete stranger who was walking past me. He did not know who I was or didn't even know if I was religious. I was so proud of this man because he was not ashamed of his beliefs. I don't care what religion you are in; you should not be ashamed of your religion.

You could be "Catholic" or you could be "Seven Days Adventist" or "Baptist" "Jehovah witness" or a "Mormon" or a "Buddhist" or "Jewish religion." We are all looking for the highest power, and I believe that is "JESUS CHRIST." Jesus Christ chooses each of us to be different, but we are all His children. I have to say this because I have seen too many things in my life, in different places that people don't respect each other's faith. Sometimes we see each other in the streets and smile, to complete strangers then start talk to each other. Everything change's when each person tells what religion they come from even when they learn each other's beliefs are so different. People's attitudes towards each other change's, and it shouldn't be like that. People should not be judged by what they believe in; it's what's inside that matters.

Has anyone heard Jesus Chris say that He didn't like you or you are better than the other person or who will die first, who will die second?

Or who is good, or who is bad? I don't think so, I never read that in the Bible that He has chosen anyone for what they believe in. Jesus loves all of us equally no matter what our faith. He even said love thy neighbor. Religion is something that we should not be judging. We should respect each other until the end of time no matter what religion anyone practices. We are loved by one God no matter the color of their skin or what race. He loves all his children until the end of time. I did some research on the Internet to see how each religion works, because I have gone into three different churches in my life, and I can't say that they do anything different. Some scream, some jump around when they feel the Holy Spirit in them, through the entire ceremony but they are still looking for Jesus, so who says they are wrong.

I don't think God would get mad at me that I went to check out different churches because I believe He is in all of them. When you pray, He is there, and I know I am praying in a different church. That doesn't mean I am praying for a different person; I am still praying to Jesus Christ. I thank Him for each day of my life because I know each day, He is part of my life. Learning is part of life. Now if you are scared to learn more then you're stuck in one position, you never learn by being close minded, only by learning to open your heart and eyes and understand other people's view. I know people have saints in their home, it's not bad to believe that Saint Anthony or Saint Barbara or a Padre Pio statue are saints who did good on this earth.

If someone believes in Jesus and has a statue of Him then who are we to laugh at them for that or judge them. That is what matters the most. The most important thing is to believing in Jesus or God's whatever name you want to call Him.

The miracles that surround us is His love and love we need to have for each other no matter what color we are or what church we belong to. We all believe in a great man who died for our sins, believing in Him is the greatest peace of mind anyone can have. I know writing this part on religion will hit people the wrong way or may be not so with this paragraph. I just wrote what I wanted to say. GOD BLESS you all. I need to point out something. When I was growing up a week before Easter, I would be watching TV. And I would watch the religious movies. Like when Jesus Christ was crucified or the 10 Commandments.

It could have been in English or Spanish even though I saw more movies in English, for me it was a tradition to see it every year. It was great the month of Easter, go sit down and watch a movie about Jesus Christ or the Ten Commandments. It did teach us about Jesus Christ, but now it's been three years going on four that I noticed something different. They don't show any movies for weeks like back in the day. If I find one movie on TV about Jesus Christ, it will be on the same day of Easter Sunday.

I know and understand there are so many different religions out there in the world, but why change something that we grow up watching. Why take it off the TV"? That is why the world is going crazy, and I know there are people who don't even believe in Jesus Christ. And I am not saying those people are bad because I am not here to judge them, I leave that to the Lord. I am asking, are we losing our religion because if you look there, are more people who believe in God then people who don't believe? Stop hurting each other. The more we judge each other, the more we are at war with one another.

Why so much hatred toward each other? We need to stand by each other as Jesus Christ stood by our side. His love for us still is unconditional. We all need to stop and look around at the children, they are the ones getting lost in all of this. Yes, your children hear and see how adults act with one another so think about it, children are the next generation. That's how I see it. It's not looking good from where I am standing. I am asked what are the children seeing in their future? I can answer that. Not believing in themselves or even losing respect toward themselves and everybody around them. I know people in the world are so busy working because there is no other choice. Think about this. If you take one hour of your time and go to church with your child it won't hurt you or if you can't make it to the church, take the Bible and pray for as long as you can. In your home, Jesus is everywhere. People let Him into their homes. Don't let the haters destroy our salvation. Bring back Jesus Christ to the front lines. Our world is being destroyed by hate, judging, and war against each other.

Think about it

Jesus Christ is waiting for His children to open their hearts to Him. While He waits, He is holding us close to Him.

We are all His children   He is holding us

God bless world

Having a dream

All my life I dreamed of having my own business. And there is a saying that if you dream for something you want and you never quit dreaming and have faith in yourself, then some way or another your dream will come true. That if you want something so bad, you don't let anything or anyone stop you from reaching your goals. I always had dreamed with different things when I was growing up. I always dreamed of having a van.

In 1998, my dream came true. It is not a big deal having a van but because I always loved vans, I wanted one. I laugh now, but I realize three years later that my dream came true, I got a van and even though wasn't new, it was one of my dream cars. Another dream was I always wanted a business, also a mobile home. I work off and on for ten years in the flea market and it was like running a business. I did not get rich, but I got enough money to pay my bills on time.

After the flea market closed after ten years, that's when I also realized that my dream did come true. I was proud of myself that I could do something I loved. I know it was not much, but I made enough money to pay off my bills and that was fine by me to get all the bills paid off on time. Knowing now that two dreams had come true. I know I can't give up. I still want to have my store. But I am happy and satisfied that I did accomplish something in my life. Even though it was a flea market, and a lot of people think it's a hobby but it's like a dream of having a store of your own; besides, you have to start somewhere. I also wanted to own a mobile home; well I hope to someday owning a mobile home. I would even be happy to just ride in one.

One day my brother Ferdie wanted to go on a vacation, he wanted to go to Virginia. Not realizing that my dream would become a reality because when my brother Ferdie rented a mobile home. During the ride my sister in law Marie said to me, "Jennie, your dream came true, you are in a "mobile home." I looked at Marie and said, "Oh yea. I see it this way." Even though I didn't buy a mobile home and just rode in one I believe as little as the dream is, people should be happy just to have something you want. Wow, how amazing it feels when a dream comes true no matter how little it is. If your mind is strong enough and you don't let anyone keep it from you, as long as it is safe. People might say you just rode in the mobile home or it was not yours to keep. I have to say no, I didn't own it, but I felt a part of my dream came true.

I have to say; everyone's dreams are different. But if it is safe and is something you want to do, go for it now. If you fail don't stop trying, who are you hurting in the long run? Keep yourself positive while you are trying to reach your dream. I had many dreams while growing up, but one dreams I didn't have was seeing Jesus Christ or writing a book. That was the last thing on my mind Period. I always thought when I die, I will see Jesus Christ. When I am 40 years old, I see Him. I have to include all the many miracle's too. I have to believe that was part of my chart before I was born. No matter what I wrote on the chart it did change my life. I have always dreamt to know my family tree. I even dream of having a family reunion getting to meet people I never met before. That's something I grew up talking about often. And dreaming of knowing my family's past but never in a million years I thought I was writing about my family, especially writing it in a book, especially about writing who had a spiritual gift.

Something I think about is never count out things that you think will never happen or can't be done. I believe it's never too late to learn new things for yourself, in the long run that is the person who you will became in your destiny, and let your faith lead you. Now quick advice to you: if you are planning to do something keep it to yourself keep quiet, until it happens. Sometimes if you tell people and they get happy for you and then your plan did not work out what happens you feel ashamed because you said something and it didn't happen right.

Just do whatever you are planning, keep it to yourself, for your own good, and then you will see it come out better than you thought! Life works in mysterious ways so don't worry about what people are going to say. If you worry about what people are going to say, then you will keep yourself from doing whatever you wanted to do in your life because you are scared of what if she or he says something to me. As for me, I'm very happy who I've become and having a spiritual gift.

Now I will say this, if this is why Jesus Christ put me on this earth to do so be it. I will do it. Now remember, keep going with your dreams and goals, and always have faith in yourself. Because in the end, you were born to do something special, no matter what it is. As long as it is good, in the end the right people who were meant to be in your life will have your back. When you're searching for whatever your dream is you have to remember it's your life so you have to be very positive about everything. My next subject is about if you want everything to work in your life then you have to be positive.

Thinking positive

There are so many people in the world that think, "oh why me," "oh look, that other person is doing better than me." Oh, I can't get a job," "oh why has this happened to me," "why, why, why." If you think negative every day or worry about others that have more than you, then you will be miserable. Stop step back, take a look inside yourself, open up your mind and heart and start thinking positive. And you will see everything in your life will change. Don't get me wrong, it will not change overnight. It will be ok, however, because sometimes we have to go through rough patches.

Then you will see that everything will work out. And you will see were your life is supposed to be at this very moment. Now that is if you keep yourself with an open mind. Keep yourself positive. Leave your life with a positive outlook at life. And if you are with your kids be happy, teach them to be positive in their life and teach them not to worry about life. Now if you worry, "Oh man, I am sick" then you will be sick. Or "Oh, I hate my job," why can't I find a better job." You can if you change your ways of thinking and stop worrying. Think about what you are sharing with your kids. Not by saying why do my children have to go through this like I have.

If you think negative, then what your children see is negative. Start talking positive, and you can change the cycle of life for your children; if not, then your children will continue the same pattern that you went through again. Sit down and try it, look deep inside your soul. Talk to your angels and ask them for help. And as soon as you give them the permission to help you, they will start helping you.

From the inside out and don't worry if you don't hear them talk to you, trust me they are helping you change, and you will notice how you start feeling the changes. Keep in mind God put the angels to help us, the universe, to work in mysterious ways. Don't get me wrong, it won't happen overnight but it will happen and if you keep yourself thinking positive everything will work out. Remember no one can think positive for you except you. You will see changes in your life, even in the way you think it will start to change. Always remember to give thanks to God for what you have today and every day.

If you have a car that is rundown at least it runs. Thank God for that too because at least you're not walking. When you want to get a good job think positive and say I will get that job, I will have the money. I will get a new car today; I will get my new house; positive thinking will get you places. So, you are the one in your life that has to stand up and say, "Ok I am going to change and no one can tell me different, I will win and this will be my year." The word "no" is not an option. It is not good to always be saying no, I can't do that change. Think, 'ok,' what can I do to change myself? Sit down and write what you want in your life. You will see how many things you will come up with.

Then write about what you don't like that are negative in your life. And you will see how many more positive things you have than negative. You will see how the good will come out more than you realized. Remember, try not to say, "I can't" and change it to, "I will." or "I can." Don't get mad if things don't work the way you want them to. Just remember,

God may have closed one door but if you look closely, you might see another open door at the right moment and maybe in a different direction that is better for you.

God will have your next door open. You will notice it and recognize that God with all His angels started to help you, and things will start getting better. Now if you are already positive, and you tell someone to be positive and they keep being negative, they are not ready yet, but don't worry, it simply is not their time for be positive. Just work on yourself, and whatever you want to you achieve, go for it. Meanwhile, don't worry about the person next to you, sooner or later they will catch up. "Don't give up on yourself!" Have faith because you will see that you are not alone in this world. Jesus Christ is holding your hand and is walking with you through it. Remember, positive is the key, and the feeling you will feel will be great. God blesses in your new journey. Meanwhile, I'm still looking for more information about my family's past. I got to know a little more detail of one family member. They used to call him, Minio, but because his nieces and nephew did not know better, and no one corrected them they called him Aunt Minio.

Still learning about Hermino

On May 22, 2008 I woke up laughing because I had a dream of my great uncle Herminio. In the dream Uncle Herminio was sitting at the kitchen table. I can't not recall who else was there with us because the only thing I remember was a lady sitting in front of me and facing Herminio. When the dream was happening at that moment, I did not know who the man was. But he spoke to me and said to me "your eyes are just like your father's" and that when I heard a voice ask him who are you. His response was, I am Uncle Herminio, but everyone knew me by Aunt Minio." Then he said to me, "Oh and by the way I want to give you my permission to put my name in your book." I woke up laughing and thought. I just dreamed about a dead guy, and I don't even know him at all and he just gave me his permission to use his name in my book.

Later that day I went to see my Uncle Edward, and I told him that I had a dream of Aunt Minio and told him about the dream. At that moment, my Uncle Edward said when my Aunt Minio was alive and he was a joker; he loved to joke around. At that moment, I needed to know more about this man. When my mother walked into the room, I asked her if she knew a little bit more about her Uncle Minio. My mother said that she only knew a little bit about him because at that time she lived in Puerto Rico. And he was living in New York but the little bit she knew was that he loved to laugh and make everyone laugh. Then my mother told me something else that on his deathbed he made his sister Blanca laugh from jokes that he told just until he died. So that's when I decided to call one of his daughters for more information.

When I called my cousin Lillian to ask her about her father, I told her about the dream. She laughed and said that was him. He liked to make people laugh; people liked him because he was upbeat and loved to laugh. I remembered Lillian told me one time that her father also had a gift. When I asked her what type of a spiritual gift he had, she told me he saw the dead people. When I asked her if it was like the Bruce Willis movie, seeing dead people, she said no, that he saw skeletons in a negative way, that he did not like his gift at all, that he didn't like talking about it. Then I asked her what kind of illness did he died from. Lillian said he was an alcoholic and died of liver cirrhosis. That did shock me because I did not know he died because of his drinking and to have a gift like the one he had; I would have gotten drunk too. My mother also told me he died eight months after his mother Conchita. My Uncle Herminio died at the age of 54 in 1971. I am grateful I see angels thank God for that. I was visiting my cousin Helen. We were talking about pictures, and I decided to look at my cousin Helen's old picture of family members. When I asked her about a picture a man, she said that was her father, Herminio. I smiled to myself never telling anyone, but to my surprise this is how I saw him in my dream. So, I took a picture with my cell phone because I had to have a copy of the man who gave me his permission after death to use his name.

So. Uncle Minio R.I.P God bless your soul and thank you for coming to me and giving one last joke.

What ever happened to the little boy?

I still wonder from time to time about the little boy that came to me the first time. Whatever happened to him? I wonder if I ever see him again the way I saw him the first time. And people still ask me if I still feel him. My answer is yes, I still feel him, and he still jumps on my bed but not every day but he makes sure I know he is still around. Also, he came to me in a dream, he told me he came from a family of three; he was the middle child, and he was nine years old when he passed away.

He even showed me a picture of himself with his two other brothers who had dark hair. He was a white boy from a middle-class family. That is the only time he gave me a message about himself. One night he was jumping on my bed, and I was really tired. And I said "Please stop jumping on my bed, I am very tired." The next thing I know I felt and heard him jump off the bed to the floor. I was amazed because I could hear him jump off then run off. I could hear his footsteps and I was like, "wow cool," but I didn't dare look his way at the time, not because I was scared, because I was tired.

I wanted to keep sleeping, but I told my mother the next day it was cool the way I heard his footsteps running off. I know people will ask me why I didn't get scared. I was more in shock hearing his footsteps and second, it's been a few years since he's been around. I got use to him jumping on my bed. Besides, he is still letting me know, he still around. I often think about him and wonder if I ever will see him again the way I saw him the first time. I wonder if I do see him if I will have the courage to talk to him.

If I do get to see him, will I try my best to ask him why he is not in heaven with the Lord. I will ask him why he is hanging out with me. Now if the day comes and if it does happen then I pray I ask God to give me the strength not to run away and speak to the kid. I have to say when I saw Jesus Christ a lot of people, I knew asked me if Jesus Christ talked to me. The answer is no, He never said a word, the only thing was when I saw the sun changed then He came toward me and then all the events that happened after that feeling His presence in me.

Also, someone also asked me if the Virgin of Guadalupe said something to me. Also, the answer is no, she stood there, and when I saw her, I also saw the sacred heart of Jesus and all the angels. The only thing I kept hearing was the voices that were all the angels telling me He was coming. If He did say something, I can't remember because when my neighbor Bertha told me, "I said he told me to do it." And like I said before I can't remember all of August. But no matter what happened I was already blessed for a new beginning. For me to know more about what I went through, I had to go back to a group that someone told me about and sounded very interesting. When I was going to them, I decided to go back to see if anyone could help, me. it is called "Metaphysical."

The Metaphysical group

I realized I had to understand more of what was happening to me. Someone told me about a group of people who meet with each other and it is called Metaphysical. These are a group of people who help each other and learn from one another. Each person has their paranormal event how they feel or see things; even though each person has a different spiritual gift, they do help each other to understand that spiritual gift. Like I said each gift is different, each one of us, not everyone hears their spirit guides. Some people can see a picture that has been showing in their head and for each person it's a different experience.

Like I said before this spiritual gift doesn't come with instructions. When I decided to go back again to the group meetings it had been a year or two since I had stopped going. When I started to hear my spiritual guide and so many other things keep happening to me, that's when I saw Jesus and every other miracle and even when I wrote all the predictions. This is one of the reasons I started to write this book. I returned to the group to see if I could learn more and if I was on the right track or if anyone else heard ghosts or felt things or heard their spirit guides.

I learned I was not the only one on this journey. Some of the people have had a spiritual gift since they were children and some from two years ago. In the group meetings, I began to understand more. I know it is not easy not to get scared because you do, you are only human, but being around people who have gone through what you are going through helps a lot.

Besides they don't judge you or look at you strangely and look beyond the skin of the person and for me I was happy to find help with these wonderful people. And for those who have this spiritual gift and sometimes feel alone because you don't know what is going on, or you feel afraid of what people would say. Like sometimes, people watching TV may say that they are fake. Or even see a person reading the palm of another person, you could hear the reaction to those are passing by, saying, "look they are freaks." Or "they are crazy" or "they are bad people" or "they are witches." No one ever put his or her self's in anyone else's shoes and think how a person is feeling or what the person has gone through.

If you feel bad when something happens and someone talks bad to you or another person, whatever people says that makes you feel bad, think about it. Even before you talk begin to think how you felt before you do the same thing to others. Remember one out of every ten people who experience paranormal things do feel out of place. Some of these people don't know who to turn to. Many after they had been rejected from their family and tried killing themselves for not knowing what was happening to them. Remember don't judge unless you walk in their shoes. Now some people are lucky because they have some help. They have family members with their own spiritual gifts.

They can learn faster by being helped by their family members and some family members are more open to it, and that is a plus for some people. Some of us are very lucky, some of us can learn by reading books you can find in book stores. At first when I was looking, I didn't know the book store has a row of bookshelves called "new age."

This was new to me. But I learned from some of the best book writers who are out there.

For those who are looking for an answer you can learn from different books. They might give you some idea if you have similar supernatural events you went through and maybe you might know what kind of gift you have. I thank God that it is 2008 because you can see that there are more people experiencing spiritual phenomena. And there are more people open to it and some people are not scared to talk about it like the 1800s or the 1900s when the people were pointed out doing something and people thought you were a bad person and called you a witch.

Today times have changed and I hope that with my book being one more for those who need help and answers for their questions. They could see and feel that they are not alone in the world. And I hope maybe your family members are more accepting. Like my mother and her brother Edward, my Aunt Maria, my brother Ferdie, his wife Marie even my brother Cesar and his wife Yalin and some close friends who know the truth. Because being judged from the start, this is why I kept some of my family members in the dark.

The reason I keep some family members in the dark it not all about the judgment, because I know they still love me. The real reason is I really didn't want to hear negative remarks. I repeat I know they love me and besides I know they will find out either way when they read this book. Anyway, I know that I do have knowledge and in due time they all will know who I am now. I repeat I know they love me and besides I know they will find out either way when they read this book.

Anyway, I know that I do have knowledge and in due time they all will know who I am now. Besides, they still know me, I am the same person they saw grow up, but different.

I am now a spiritual reader, who is helping people with the help of Jesus Christ and His angels. They still know me. I was never a person who made a joke about religion. Or lie about something like this by saying I saw the most powerful man in the world, Jesus Christ. I won't lie about something as big as this. I am not a person that cries wolf. I am the same person that they saw grow up and love. The only difference is I do feel different. I have grown to feel more at peace with myself and I know I love life more than ever. The only difference about me is I have a special ability that I honor and respect. Plus, my favorite part is it came with the blessing of Jesus Christ Himself.

How can you have more of a blessing than that? I should never have kept a big secret like this. Because what I saw was a wonderful man that we all know and grew up with, and prayed to. Plus, He died for our sins. "Yes Jesus Christ" like I said I should never have kept a secret like this from my family at all. But at the time I was scared of the judging and in my case, I didn't know who to run to or talk to. When I could not hold it any longer, I had to speak up. And I picked the people who I thought would back me up. At least I have a handful that I can talk to and who will not judge me. Besides, I could not keep it any longer and yes, I was very scared.

That's something I think about every day. When the rest of the family learned of my secret what would they say or how would they react to it after reading this book. I came to realize I don't think about it anymore. I keep going with my life by doing spiritual readings for people and by helping them connect with their dead family members and by helping the people that I read, maybe I help them heal their heart. I know if I did that then I did a good job for God.

Besides, without Him I would have never been able to connect with my spirit guide or the dead family members and I thank God that He gave me a job to work for Him. I know some people want to learn more from the spiritual world. And I have to say it takes time and one must have the passion. Now that you have this ability's is like going back to school and taking time to learn and understand that it is not you in control. Is in God and His angels' hands. Remember what they give you is what you need Now that you have this ability's is like going back to school and taking time to learn and understand that it is not you in control. Is in God and His angels' hands. Remember what they give you is what you need to learn a little bit at a time. And how you do learn from it is new, each time is different. Or when you read people you want to make sure you are helping in the right way.

By not putting your thoughts into the reading but just asking the person you are going to read not to tell you, anything that keeps them quiet until you finish reading them. That's how I do it and that's why I don't want to put anything the person said into the reading. And when I read people, I even get surprised by what the spirit says. I do tell the person that I read if that happens to tell me.

It's funny when the person comes back to you and says that what you told them came true. A lot of times I even get surprised by what I am about to say because I know I was not thinking about it. Remember learn every step, remember to try focusing on what your guide is telling you to do and say to help the people that need the reading. Remember what I have to say is I'm not saying that if Jesus didn't choose you to be a spiritual healer or any other kind of gift that you are not special because you are.

Jesus did put each one of us with something special. I give you a few examples. You can play baseball, become a famous baseball player, or some can be a poet or a lawyer or a doctor or a movie star. See no matter what God chooses us to do or we choose before we are born, it doesn't mean you are not special. We are all God's children. You were born for a good reason and no matter how bad it gets, there is a light at the end of the tunnel. There are a lot of people in this world with a different story. It could be sad, or it could be great. You could come from a family that been abused. Or you can come out of a family that is poor or a family that is rich but you can be the one who comes out on top because you need to find your calling to do well in life. By being hurt, being angry or being negative from your experience doesn't mean you won't become someone you want to be.

Show yourself that whatever you want you can do and can have it. Don't get me wrong because some dreams change in a different direction. I give you another example. Some people want to become a police officer. Maybe they can't pass the exam. For one reason or another but some reason, you can do something you never thought of doing.

Like becoming a movie star or becoming a doctor or just the best that, you can be. Think about what life has for you.

There are ups and downs but, in the end, it is you the one looking back and being happy with what you have done with no regret. With the help of Jesus of course and if you think you didn't get His help then that is your choice too because I can't judge you for that. Try to understand what Jesus gives you is never a curse. It is a learning experience and understanding is in your chart you wrote before you were born.

Besides, you have to deal with it and learn from all of it and in the end, you can understand by looking back and saying what you did is good.

Through it, all, you run into people who you can learn from, and there are some people who just pass you by just to touch your soul. And there are other people who come to stay to show you a little more of your journey. Like me, I learn from good friends Pam, Jennifer, Doreen, and a few others who did cross my life. At this very moment when I needed help or needed the healing, God did give me people when I needed them the most. Remember this is a journey that we all go through one step at a time with God's help. We are all His angels working on earth.

Doreen's story

I keep learning my ability and my spiritual guide keeps helping me out in my life by telling my predictions. In the meantime, I keep going to the group Metaphysical. And I became friends with Pamela Sayre, and in the group, I also met Doreen Wales and Jennifer Thomas and a few others. I keep meeting good people and become good friends with some. Sometimes I hear people say that people that are psychic are not religious. Oh, man, so many people are so wrong while I learn in this metaphysical group everyone, I meet has their religious belief.

No matter if Jesus or different Gods but they do have their religion in their way. But even though some come from different religions I know that we are not that different. In ours believe in Jesus or God because in the end religion is believing one divinity, the almighty Jesus Christ. Everyone in the world has a different belief. We are all different people in this world. No matter what we are all God's children with a spiritual gift whether or not we believe in Him.

I decided to invite a friend Doreen Wales to my apartment. We sat down and began to talk about dreams when Doreen told me a dream she had, and I'd like to share this dream in her words. It was a difficult time in Doreen's life. She'd just had a child, Alan, and Doreen went home and began crying herself to sleep and praying for help. When Doreen heard a voice calling her name, she recognized the voice but at the time did not know who it was, but knew it was familiar. She was completely asleep; she began the dream that would change her life, and it started. "I was dreaming I was driving a car with my sister's friend Abby, and no matter how hard I tried the car would not go forward.

Abby acted and kept talking like a real-life Abby, was always in crisis and always threatening suicide and cussing Mom and others for things that she was doing. While I tried to move the car forward Abby kept talking and talking. I wanted to get out and drop her off quickly. Then all of a sudden, the car went forward and the dream changed from being in the country to the city. We stopped in front of a high rise with revolving doors, and I got out of the car and went through the revolving doors. There was a beautiful park. In my dream, I am watching policemen circle a young man after they had shot him down. Now no one stopped to help this man and I started screaming and running and saying, "Doesn't anyone care?"

As I kept running screaming I kept running and ended up through another building. Then I saw a white-robed man. His back was toward me; he was speaking to a crowd of people. I collapsed at the sight of him still crying, "Doesn't anyone care?" He turned looked at me, I know without words, He said, "I care." I got up calmly, walked back through the building to the park and building and got in the car with Abby. I felt love and I felt calm. I'm changed forever. When I woke up, I looked at my husband and as I kept looking at him my thoughts were, that was Jesus Christ, and I kept looking at my husband. And said no he wouldn't believe me and well I also didn't believe that Jesus Christ talked to me. I got up and as I was walking by the phone my friend Theresa called. We had not spoken in more than twenty years, and the first thing she said was, "Why don't you believe He would not come to you?" I was unable to answer I was so shocked that she called me. At the same time, I dreamed my dream, and when I was walking by the phone, it would be her making sure I would not think otherwise.

The day I went to a meeting, and a woman said to me, "Why don't you believe Jesus will come to you?" It was not a regular meeting, then I was shocked I recognized the voice that I heard before. A few of these women and I often pray together as a group. They told me, "We were worried about you last night at 6:30 p.m." Those where the voices that called my name. Then a woman looked at me and said, "Why don't you believe Jesus wouldn't come to you?" I know I can't doubt. I went to a spiritual priest and told him the story, and the priest said, God or Jesus Christ does not appear to people." Why would a priest say that, I wondered? When Doreen told me her story, I know the truth about my life; it was changed forever and I am so happy. As I heard Doreen tell me her story, my hair stood up. As Doreen finished telling her story I responded by telling Doreen my story. That I too had seen Jesus Christ come to me and after everything was over, I told Doreen I also went to the church to talk to a priest. The reaction of that priest was cold, while I was giving him my testimony to what I saw and felt and what happened to me. If a priest's reaction was that way then, I can't imagine what regular people will say. Then what happened to the faith of all humans if a person who is preaching the word of the Lord and their reaction is like that? Then what will happen to a human on this earth? We are all losing our hope in miracles and answers to what people hope for. The reaction of people who I told was happier than if I'd won the lottery. And that's how I feel: I won the lottery. It's not money but it is more than that, it's a sight of seeing Jesus and the feeling of peace that few people ever felt. I never thought to experience such a miracle that this next story was more of a healing to Yaya's heart.

Yaya's story

On June 14, 2008 I went to the Bronx, New York City. Matter of fact that's where my family is from. I decided to go to my Uncle Rafael's 70th birthday party. The reason I wanted to go was to see if I could get more information from the family history. Now what was more of a surprise to me was, I went to my Uncle Rafael's daughter, Yaya's house; we were getting ready for bed. We began to talk for a couple of hours that night. My mother and I heard the story of what happened to her and she began to tell us that after her mother Gladys passed away ten years ago that she began to lose it, she was crying all the time. She felt lost without her mother and she began to pray and pray to Jesus to help her. She felt so much sorrow with her mom gone and she felt so alone. One night she went to bed at 2:30 a.m. she awoke to see, on the wall, Jesus looking back at her. The next thing she knows when she looks in the mirror in her bedroom, she did not see her face she kept seeing Jesus Christ's face instead of hers. That's when she says she realized her mother was resting in peace, and now she feels a peace that she never felt before. She was saying how happy she is and she loves to hear Gospel music everyday as much as possible. My mother began to tell her about my miracles that happened to me and of course I finished the story by crying. I also told my cousin Yaya that I also feel at peace. That was when Yaya turned around toward her Aunt Nellie, when she that when she walked up to the car to greet us when she looked at me. She could tell something was different in my face. I smiled because it was not the first time someone had said that about me.

I came to realize Jesus showed each one of us in different forms of miracles and we can't deny that He is always there when we need Him the most. I did learn my journey has begun. While my book is coming to and ending I still want to say for those who are that reading this book thank you for your support by reading my book and understanding that no matter where you are and whatever situation you get yourself into you always can count on Jesus and the angels to take care of you. I'm still learning from all the predictions I wrote. Some already did come out like the Red Sox won in 2007. And my brother Cesar and his wife Yamir Mendez moved away, and my cousin Edward Rivera and his girlfriend Monique Ocasio will be having a baby.

To my surprise I thought the prediction I wrote was more to the future like for 2015 and beyond. I thought it was further into the future. But to my surprise some did come out. I did learn that predictions don't have time or limits. I guess I am learning that by experience. And by going to the group Metaphysical, to go to all meetings. I began to make a few friends like Pam and Doreen and Jennifer and a few others who helped me understand this is a special gift that God gave me. Even though I am helping people now, I have more reason to keep helping them. Some people need to understand we are regular people who happen to experience paranormal things in our lives'. I try to do my everyday routine by writing my book or if someone want me to read them, I try to my best ability to help them heal.

But beside that I am a regular person who wants to have fun in life. Even though sometime I have to understand this gift was to me.

For many reasons I stopped asking why me and go with the flow; besides, without the help of Jesus and my guide, Theresa, I would not be able to do what I do best, which is to help people heal. Thanks again for my spirit guide. I know this is the beginning of my journey in my life, and I am grateful that it will be a wonderful future for me and everyone else with whom I cross paths.

Looking back on the family tree

I keep searching for my family history and I keep learning from the past. I found out that my great great-great grandmother Eliza Muñez had her gift and still she also helped people with herbs. I even found out her sister also had a gift, though as to exactly what kind I don't know. But to learn that there was a history of family members who had a spiritual gift was enlightening. It is good to know that I was not the only one. Now it did jump many generations and no one knows if any of the family members were brave enough to use their spirituality by reading someone. Or if they were scared to work with it or if someone told them not to. I wonder if my great-great grandmother and her mother Eliza Muñez ever knew any predictions.

If they did? Did they ever get the guts to tell anyone anything? Thinking about it, like I said before those were the days when people wanted to quite their gift and besides, they were in the closet back then. I always wanted to know my family tree since I could remember I never knew why no one else was interested in knowing the family tree, that I know. Since I wrote this book, I realize that I did go back only to my great great-great grandmother Eliza Muñez and great-great grandmother Conchita Hernandez. I don't know who was Eliza's mother? It will be good to know since Eliza's died at the age of 125 or 130-year-old. Someone also said she was interviewed by the newspaper in Puerto Rico because she could remember everything that happened in the past one hundred years. It is nice to know more information about my family past.

It is nice to know if anyone else could have been a medium or a psychic. Now I know a little bit of my mother's side of the family. The problem is because my mother lost her father at an early age; we don't know his side of his family at all. I wonder if his family had a special gift. We will never know so this one I will wonder for a long time. I guess I leave it in God's hands. Or I find out more information little by little because I am so curious in everything I do. I guess I will keep searching.

Advice

I always wonder looking back when I was in the Job Corps in Bangor, Maine in 1989 or even when I was in the flea market in New Hampshire. When people keep coming up to me for advice what was the reason. I wondered if God was putting me in a spot to get me ready for what was to come. I laugh now but for me I thought maybe the person wanted get stuff off their chest. I did give people advice not knowing if I did the right thing. Every time I told someone something like, "Don't worry you will get your money." I didn't even know if they will get it in time or not. But everything came out ok, they got their money in time. Even though each advice was different back then I was in shock because every time someone came back saying their problem was solved and thank me for helping them. I guess Jesus was putting me in a position for me to get ready for the bigger journey by giving messages to people. The most important thing is to give to His children a message of love. And giving people the faith and the healing, they are looking for and I believe we need to love one another and we all still need miracle's in our life. And if I give a message of love through spiritual reading then I will do it with pleasure and to those people that had asked me for advice back then God bless you all in your journey. I want to thanks Jesus for the people who I meet in my life and those who are going to be in my future. I wish you all health and prosperity in your life.

PREDICTIONS

1. The Red Sox will win the World Series four years straight in a row breaking their record. After the Red Sox win four years in a row, they will win three more times in the years 2018, 2019 and 2020
2. The HOLLYWOOD sign will fall.
3. Earth quake will hit New Hampshire by the year 2015
4. New York City will be falling apart from a Tornado by 2025
5. Earth quake will hit around the country full force that we will not know what hit us.
6. If I am getting this right, there will be two more wars.
7. The economy will hit rock bottom for eight straight years.
8. Fuel prices will go back down from to $4.95 after President Bush
9. Tsunami will be hitting the heart of Japan and it will shock the nation to the core by year 2016

My Final thought

I want to thank God to make this final page possible, but I also want to thank my angels and guides as they continue helping me since 2007. I want to explain something. Some of us go through life not knowing what our path is. And we continue to struggle with our life but if by any chance you found your path then go all the way. God is one hundred percent behind you. To my reader I want to point out, if by any chance I help anyone with any answers you were looking for, whichever answer you found could have been spiritual or religion, either one I hope you got the answer you deserve. This is the reason I wrote this book, to help someone that might need the answers. Besides, I wanted to tell my story, and second there could have been someone out there lost as I was with nowhere to run or hide or no one to turn to like what happened to me. Final note: My journey has just started, and I accept this gift with a promise to Jesus Christ. I will do everything in my power to make Him happy with the work He gave me to do here; besides, I chose to go along for the ride. What Jesus Christ showed me was wonderful, and I know and let you all know my path has only just started. And it's a long road ahead of me, and it is a great one. Let me say my mission just began and just maybe my story is just getting started so be aware.

To be continued

LET THE "LIGHT" OF JESUS LIGHT YOUR WAY

THANK YOU AND GOD BLESS

IN THE MEMORY OF

Jesus Christ

And

Luciano Vazquez

Conchita Hernandez

Eliza Muñez

Blanca Andujar Her grandchildren called

Her Mamamita

My Best Friend

Deborah McCall

And her brother

Willie McCall

And

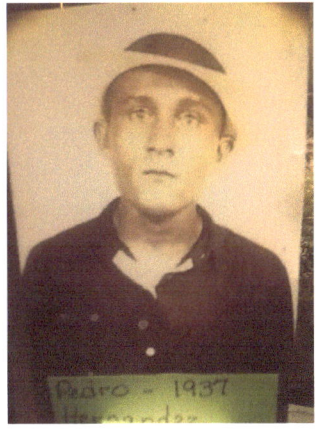

Pedro Hernadez

This picture was shown for the first time in 2013 in a family reunion no one at the reunion had ever seen it before

www.ingramcontent.com/pod-product-compliance
Lightning Source LLC
Chambersburg PA
CBHW041619220426
43661CB00046B/1501